Stencilling
for the first time™

Stencilling
for the first time™

Rebecca Carter

Sterling Publishing Co., Inc.
New York
A Sterling/Chapelle Book

Chapelle Ltd.

Owner: Jo Packham

Editor: Leslie Ridenour

Staff: Ann Bear, Areta Bingham, Kass Burchett, Marilyn Goff, Holly Hollingsworth, Will Jones, Susan Jorgensen, Barbara Milburn, Linda Orton, Karmen Quinney, Cindy Stoeckl, Gina Swapp, Sara Toliver

Special Thanks

Several projects in this book were created with outstanding and innovative products provided by the following manufacturers and retailers: **Provo Craft** of Provo, Utah, for the wide variety of products used as stencilling surfaces—cardboard snap boxes, wood products, tinware, glass containers—as well as a wide variety of stencils. Thank you Robert; **DecoArt** for stencil brushes, acrylic paints, and stencil paints. Your prompt response and willingness to provide quality products are much appreciated. Thank you Rosemary.

Library of Congress Cataloging-in-Publication Data

Carter, Rebecca.
    Stencilling for the first time / Rebecca Carter.
        p.   cm.
    "A Sterling/Chapelle book."
    Includes index.
    ISBN 0-8069-4485-4 Hardcover
        1-4027-0812-2 Paperback
    1. Stencil work. I. Title.

  TT270.C37 2000
  745.7'3--dc21   00-030818

10 9 8 7 6 5 4 3 2 1

A Sterling/Chapelle Book

First paperback edition published in 2003 by
Sterling Publishing Co., Inc.
387 Park Avenue South, New York, NY 10016
© 2000 by Rebecca Carter
Distributed in Canada by Sterling Publishing
c/o Canadian Manda Group, One Atlantic Avenue, Suite 105
Toronto, Ontario, Canada M6K 3E7
Distributed in Great Britain by Chrysalis Books
64 Brewery Road, London N7 9NT, England
Distributed in Australia by Capricorn Link (Australia) Pty Ltd.
P.O. Box 704, Windsor, NSW 2756, Australia

Printed in China
All Rights Reserved

Sterling ISBN 0-8069-4485-4 Hardcover
           1-4027-0812-2 Paperback

If you have any questions or comments, please contact:

Chapelle Ltd., Inc.
P.O. Box 9252
Ogden, UT 84409
Phone: (801) 621-2777
FAX: (801) 621-2788
e-mail: Chapelle@chapelleltd.com
website: www.chapelleltd.com

For a catalog or more information on products by Rebecca Carter, please contact:

Designs by Rebecca
P.O. Box 1295
Bountiful, UT 84011-1295
Phone: (801) 292-6624
FAX: (801) 423-3219
website: www.dbrcrafts.com

Images on pages 40 and 47 Copyright © 1999 Little Images photography by Rebecca

About the Author

Growing up in Bountiful, Utah, Rebecca Carter was the only daughter in her family of nine children. She grew up in a very close neighborhood with plenty of children to play with. Many fond memories are still felt when she returns to visit her family and friends. "I can still hear the laughter of the children playing softball in the circle and kick-the-can that was played late at night."

Rebecca's mother always said that there is never an end to learning and just recently took first place in the Bountiful Chapter of the Utah Poetry Society with her poem "Paper Bird." She enrolled Rebecca in calligraphy at the age of fourteen, which gave her many opportunities in school and within the community. Art was also a passion and Rebecca enrolled in many Saturday classes at the University of Utah during high school. She was a Sterling Scholar in art during her senior year, and she received a four-year scholarship to Southern Utah University.

Rebecca enrolled in almost every type of class that involved working with her hands. They ranged from ceramics to sculpture, to lithograph, to weaving. She graduated with a degree in fine art and a three-year degree in interior design.

After graduating from college, she taught calligraphy and watercolor classes and worked at a local craft store. An opportunity came to work as a corporate designer, so she moved her family from Cedar City to Provo. Rebecca now works as a free-lance artist for many companies.

Rebecca is married to her best friend, Rick, who is her biggest support and fan. When he's not taking care of the kids during the day, he spends his time creating recipes for cooking or working on taxidermy. They both work at home to raise their four children, Rachel, Tyrel, Chantry, and Sophie, who fill their lives with challenges, but more importantly, pure happiness.

Rebecca's newest hobby and addiction is photography. She has always loved the art, but never tried it until recently. It has opened up a whole new world of creativity. "My mother was right. There is never an end to learning. Life is an endless journey of opportunity. It is up to you what you do with it. Embrace it! In turn, it will give back to you in ways you may never have imagined."

Rebecca

Table of Contents

Stencilling for the First Time
8

Section 1: Stencilling Basics
10

What do I need to get started?
12

Section 2: Techniques 28

How do I accomplish basic stencilling using a single overlay stencil?

How do I use more than one paint color with a bridged stencil?

How do I accomplish basic stencilling with a textured ground?

How do I use stencils with registration marks?

How do I use other objects as stencils?

How do I add shading to the stencilling?

How do I use ink pads with stencils?

How do I cut my own stencil?

How do I create plaid effects using a stencil?

How can I alter the design of my stencil?

How do I mirror stencil designs?

How do I use component stencils?

How do I use theorem stencils?

How can I stencil a wall border?

Stencilling for the first time

Introduction

"Stencilling" is the process of applying paint through an opening cut out of a stiff, paint-resistant material to create a crisp, precise design.

Stencilling is an old-world art that is enjoying a modern revival. As a craft, stencilling is very appealing because it is relatively easy and it is hand-done, allowing you to express your own creativity. Stencilling gives you the freedom to create decorative schemes which will have an individuality that cannot be matched by any mass-produced paper or fabric designs.

Historically, stencilled patterns reflected the surroundings of those who chose to decorate their living spaces in this manner. For example, early American settlers used motifs such as leaves, birds, bells, and the pineapple.

Today, because there are wide varieties of stencils and paints available on the market, the possibilities for stencilling are limited only by one's own imagination.

Many of us live in houses that are uniform in design and appearance. We surround ourselves with objects that are very much like those belonging to our neighbor. Function too often takes priority over individuality. Stencilling provides a medium for personalizing and creating unique interiors and accessories that can be as sophisticated or simple, as coordinated or full of contrast as you desire. Because it offers this kind of freedom, stencilling is an excellent decorating technique.

Stencilling does not require long hours of practice—anyone can do it. Unlike freehand painting, the design does not have to be drawn first and there are no brush strokes to master. To stencil successfully, all you need to do is make certain that the surface is suitable for the chosen type of paint and that the design is suited to the room or object you want to decorate. Measure and plan your design before you begin and use one or more very light applications of the paint.

While it may take a bit longer to prepare the stencils, the time involved in completing the actual design is cut down significantly when compared to freehand painting. This is especially true when the design is to be repeated many times over a large surface or on several surfaces.

Stencils are versatile. They can be used for interior decorating—applying designs to walls, furniture, fabric, etc. They can also be used to embellish gifts and accessories such as jewelry boxes, frames, flowerpots, and floor cloths.

Take care not to overlook the potential of a single stencil. As you stencil more and more, you may begin thinking you should use more than one stencil in a room to achieve more diversity in your design. However, if you were to take on a room with only one stencil and one color of paint, you would still be able to come up with something unique by interpreting the spaces and the surfaces around you in a variety of ways. You could also take the same stencil and use it in different ways and with different paint colors in other parts of your house.

Stencils guarantee accurate and consistent results, as the time spent in initial planning combined with correct placement almost removes the chance of error and ensures the same results with each repeat.

Finally, stencils are economical in terms of both time and money spent. For example, the cost of paint and one or two stencils to decorate a room is much less than that of several rolls of wallpaper and matching textiles.

How to Use this Book

For the person who is stencilling for the first time, this book provides a comprehensive guide to supplies, techniques, and surfaces that can be used to create great decorative effects.

Section 1 familiarizes you with the basic tools and supplies you need to begin stencilling. Section 2 begins with the most basic technique—how to use a single overlay stencil. The second technique builds upon what you have already learned, adding the use of more paint colors to a bridged single overlay stencil. Each subsequent technique continues in this manner, introducing a new technique and building on the last. If you decide to jump ahead out of sequence, you may find you have skipped a technique you now need to use.

Section 3 introduces ideas for stencilling on various surfaces, using the previously learned techniques.

Finally, Section 4 provides a gallery of designs done by artists and professionals in the field. These photographs demonstrate the fabulous effects that can be achieved through the art of stencilling and will inspire you on to creating your own masterpieces.

The intent of this book is to provide a starting point and teach basic skills. The more you stencil, the more comfortable you will feel. Allow yourself a reasonable amount of time to complete your first project—remember this is your first time. You will soon discover that the stencilling techniques are easy to master.

After you have completed the first few projects, you will be surprised by how quickly you will be able to finish the remaining projects. Take pride in the talents you are developing and the unique designs only you can create.

Section 1: *stencilling basics*

What do I need to get started?

Getting Started

There are no absolutes in stencilling, but the following guidelines can help you achieve a consistent, balanced technique.

First, choose a stencil design that is pleasing to you and that will suit the project. Second, choose the type and colors of paint that will work best on the selected surface. Then make certain you have plenty of applicators to complete the design.

Make certain to purchase quality materials. After your initial investment in stencils, applicators, and paints, you will find that the stencils are virtually indestructible, provided they are properly looked after, and can be used again and again.

Stencils

Stencils can be made of brass or heavy cardstock, but are most commonly made of a thin plastic film known as mylar. They are available in all different shapes and sizes. There are stencils for large projects such as mural art, floor designs, and wall borders. There are also stencils for wood projects and small projects such as greeting cards. Those made from brass can be used for paper embossing as well. The following is a description of the different types of stencils:

Single Overlay Stencil: This stencil is the most basic in design and can also be referred to as a template. The stencil is usually made up of simple shapes such as hearts, stars, or circles without any bridges.

This simple shape stencil can be used artistically with a little know-how in basic lighting—dark recedes into the picture or design (usually along the stencil edge) and light images come forward. Always place light against dark and dark against light.

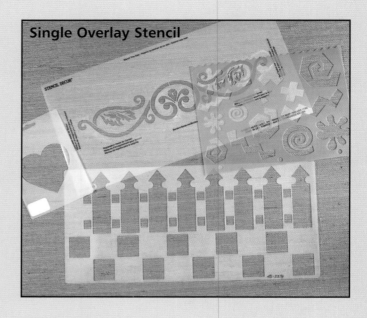

Single Overlay Stencil

Bridged Stencil: This is the most commonly used stencil. It is the most readily available and easiest to use. This stencil is referred to as a "one part" stencil because all the design elements are contained within the one stencil—often connected by bridges or spaces between the openings. A bridged stencil is as valuable in creating a beautiful design as are the multi-overlay and theorem stencils that are used in more advanced projects.

A bridged stencil is less expensive than a theorem stencil and requires simple, one-step application. However, if more than one color is used to complete the design, take care not to apply a color where it is not wanted. The bridges are very thin.

Do not be fooled by the simplicity of this type of stencil as there are endless ways to vary the design, such as taping off certain elements, flipping it for a mirrored image, or shading the paint colors. As you become more proficient in using a bridged stencil, you will want to display your finished projects in the prominent places in your home.

Bridged Stencil

Component Stencil: Any of the previously mentioned stencils can be a component stencil if it is used with other stencils, each providing a separate motif, to create an entire scene. The Garden Lamp on page 58 demonstrates how to use motifs such as flowers, flowerpots, a dirt mound, and a spade as components to create a gardening scene.

Component Stencil

Stencil with Registration Marks: Registration marks are small holes punched from a stencil. They help assure even spacing for horizontal and vertical placement of repeats and indicate how to line up successive overlays.

To mark the registration marks, slide a self-adhesive note under the hole in the stencil, making certain the note is not showing through any stencil openings. Using a pencil, mark through the hole onto the note. Repeat for all registration marks on the stencil. After stencilling is completed, simply remove the marked notes.

Multi-overlay Stencil: This type of stencil is cut from pieces of mylar and layered—one layer per color to ensure quick and exact color placement. The finished project looks like it was completed with a bridged stencil as the stencil is commonly cut with bridges or spaces between the openings. Each layer contains registration marks for ease in lining up each consecutive layer.

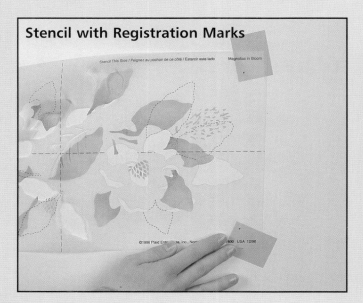

Stencil with Registration Marks

Multi-overlay Stencil

STENCIL DECOR®

Theorem Stencil: Like the multi-overlay stencil, a theorem stencil is cut from pieces of mylar and layered. However, the theorem stencil is cut so design elements are placed without bridges or spaces between the openings. Each layer of mylar is a numbered stencil and contains a different opening or part of the design. Each numbered stencil also has registration marks or a horizontal centering line for ease in lining up each consecutive overlay. When stencilled in numerical order, each layer builds upon the last to create the complete design. This process results in an artistic, hand-painted look.

Theorem Stencil

Cutting Your Own Stencil: Although there are many different stencils available, sometimes the stencil design needs to be customized to suit your project. Fabric used for home decor is a wonderful source for creating an original stencil design. For example, copy a grape cluster motif that is on a throw pillow and repeat it on the wall. Clip art and rubber-stamped images can also be enlarged and used as patterns for making stencils. For cutting your own stencils you will need:

Craft knife and swivel knife with new blades
   or an electric stencil cutter
Glass cutting mat
Light table
Pencil
Permanent marking pen
Stencil blank or sheet of mylar
Tracing paper

Determine the type of stencil that will be cut. For a bridged stencil, each element of the design must be cut in its own self-contained area. For a theorem stencil, each element is cut separately and then layered into place with the help of registration marks. Using the permanent marking pen, trace a design from fabric or clip art onto the stencil blank or sheet of mylar. Place the traced design on a glass cutting mat and cut out the designs using the craft knife for straight lines and the swivel knife for curves.

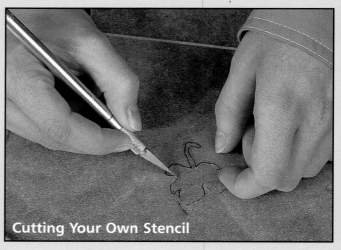

Cutting Your Own Stencil

An electric stencil cutter, which actually melts the stencil blank or mylar, can also be used to cut out the design. It is held and used like a pencil. It is very hot and melts whatever it touches. For a smooth line, take care not to stop in the middle of it.

Practice using these tools as each has its advantages and disadvantages and is difficult to control at first. Start with very simple shapes and then move on to more complex designs.

Glaze

Stencil Creme

Acrylic Paint

Outdoor Paint

Air-dry Enamel Paint

Ink Pad

Paints

There are several types of paint that can be used for stencilling. Each type of paint has its advantages and disadvantages. Therefore, one paint may work better than another on a particular project.

Stencil Creme: The creamy consistency of this paint makes it so it will not seep under the stencil. The edges of the finished design are crisp. Since the creme stays moist, the shading, highlighting, and blending process is made easy.

Use a small amount of the paint on a disposable palette. This allows for more flexibility in blending colors and provides a cleaner, larger area to work with without the clutter of the paint jars. Note: The creme is self-sealing—when the container is opened you will notice a film over the surface. Simply remove this film with a twist of a paper towel.

Advantages:
• The creme will not seep under the stencil, leaving a clean, crisp design.
• Stencil creme goes a long way and, subsequently, will last a very long time.
• The creme stays wet longer, making blending, shading, and mixing colors very easy.
• It can be used on fabric, wood, tin, walls, and paper.

Disadvantages:
• This oil-based creme takes longer to dry. Take care when removing the stencil and repeating not to smear the stencilled design.

- The cure time for fabric stencilled with the creme is two weeks. If it is heat-set for at least 30 seconds, the fabric can be washed within 48 hours.

Recommended Applicators:
  Fabric dye brushes
  Stencil brushes

Clean-up:
  Soap and water

Note: After the stencilling is completed on wood or tin projects and before continuing the repeat, mist the design with matte acrylic spray. Allow it to dry and then reposition the stencil.

Acrylic Paint: This medium is commonly used for basic stencilling, such as checkerboards and textured backgrounds, on wood and tin. This paint dries quickly. It is not recommended for shading as the colors do not blend easily. Practice, using a small amount of acrylic paint to avoid seepage.

Advantages:
- Acrylic paint is widely available.
- This type of paint provides great, quick coverage for simple backgrounds.
- The paint dries quickly.

Disadvantages:
- The consistency of this paint is not very thick and it has a tendency to seep under the stencil's edge.
- Again, because of the fast drying time, the paint colors do not blend easily.
- Textile medium must be used with acrylic paint for use on fabric.

Recommended Applicators:
  Fabric dye brushes
  Makeup sponges

Clean-up:
  Soap and water

Air-dry Enamel Paint: Air-dry enamel paint is formulated specifically for glass and nonporous surfaces. It can be used on dishes, glassware, vases, candleholders, etc. The consistency is thinner than that of acrylic paints and tends to be "sticky"—especially when layering the paint.

Advantages:
- This is a very durable paint.
- The paint dries quickly.
- After baking, the paint is dishwasher safe.

Disadvantages:
- Curing time before washing is seven days.
- The sticky consistency of the paint makes it difficult to use—especially for beginners.
- This paint has a tendency to seep under certain types of stencils.
- It tends to stick to certain types of stencils if left on for any length of time.
- It is difficult to clean off stencils.
- Because the paint is fast-drying, blending colors is difficult.

Recommended Applicators:
  Makeup sponge

Clean-up:
  Stencil cleaner or soap and water

Glaze: This paint is thick and easy to apply to most surfaces. It has a creamy consistency and covers well in one or two coats. It is great for decorating walls and fabric. It works well with texturing techniques such as rolling, stencilling, and sponging. When glaze is used on fabric, the paint must be heat-set.

Advantages:
- This versatile paint can be used alone or mixed with acrylic paint.
- Glaze will not seep under stencils.
- It is slow-drying and easy to control.

Disadvantage:
- There are not many colors to choose from.

Recommended Applicators:
  Large flat brush for base coat
  Makeup sponge and stencil roller for stencilling

Clean-up:
  Soap and water while paint is still wet

Ink Stamp Pad: An ink stamp pad is most commonly used for the craft of rubber stamping. Its pigment is highly concentrated and it is available in single or multiple color pads, making it ideal for quick stencilling. This colored ink should be applied in several light layers. Colors such as bright yellow and hot pink can be toned down by adding very light layers of brown.

Advantages:
• An array of multiple colors are available in a single ink stamp pad.
• The ink is clean and easy to apply to the project.

Disadvantages:
• The ink takes longer to dry than some paints. Care must be taken when removing the stencil and repeating the design.
• Compared to other paints, there are not many colors available.
• The ink colors are more difficult to blend.

Recommended Applicators:
  Cotton swabs
  Sponge daubers

Clean-up:
  Water

Outdoor Paint: This paint is new to the craft industry, but offers the ability to take stencilled projects outdoors. Stencilled pots, decks, and concrete walkways will beautify any yard.

   The consistency of this paint is similar to that of acrylic paint, but it tends to be somewhat slicker. When applied in several light layers, it does not seep under the stencil very easily. Allow 3–4 hours for it to cure.

Advantages:
• This is a wonderfully durable paint that withstands the elements.
• Outdoor paint is easily applied to various surfaces.
• This paint does not seep under the stencil.
• It is a fast-drying paint.

Disadvantages:
• The consistency of this paint is sticky and needs to dry between applications.
• Because the paint is fast-drying, blending colors is difficult.

Recommended Applicators:
  1" flat brush for base coat
  Makeup sponge for stencilling

Clean-up:
  Soap and water

Stencil Gel: Stencil gel is a semitranslucent paint that is easy to control and blend. The thick consistency of this paint minimizes seeping and smudges. It is colorfast when used on fabric. It is also nontoxic and water-based, making for quick clean-up.

Advantages:
• Thick consistency minimizes seeping.
• The water-based gel makes for easy clean-up.

Disadvantages:
• Compared to other paints, there are not many colors available.

Recommended Applicators:
  Makeup sponges
  Sponge daubers
  Sponge pouncers
  Stencil brushes

Clean-up:
  Soap and water

Miscellaneous Paint Mediums: You may also want to try gel stains, chalks, pastel crayons, and food coloring.

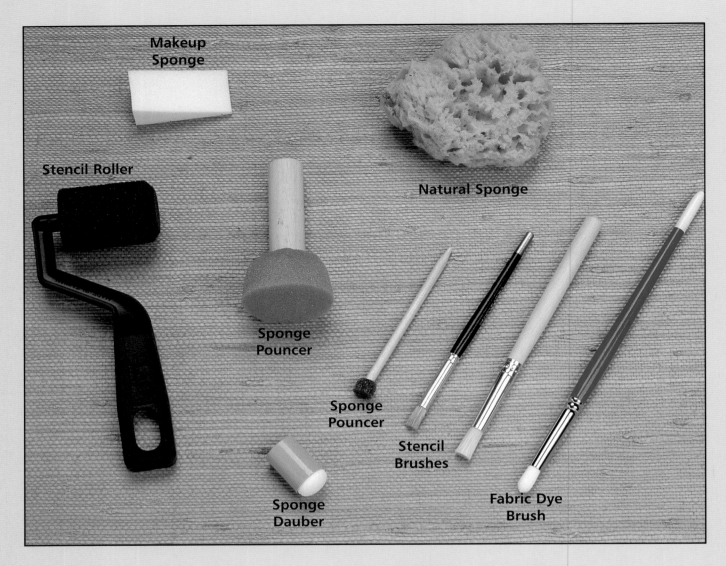

Makeup Sponge

Stencil Roller

Natural Sponge

Sponge Pouncer

Sponge Pouncer

Stencil Brushes

Fabric Dye Brush

Sponge Dauber

Applicators

An applicator is used to apply the paint into the openings of the stencil. Initially, the applicator you choose will depend on what is called for in the project instructions. However, as you experiment with different kinds of applicators, you will come to decide which is best for you. The choices available for stencilling range from traditional stencil brushes to stipple brushes, to sponges, to stencil rollers. Some applicators work better than others with certain paints and some even produce a particular texture. The best applicator for the job is most often a matter of personal preference.

Stencil Brush: A stencil brush is round with a flat head of either very soft or very stiff bristles. This brush is the most commonly used for stencilling and is available in a variety of sizes. Use the brush size most appropriate for the stencil you have chosen.

Fabric Dye Brush: This brush is also known as a stipple brush. It is round with a dome-shaped head. It has soft bristles and is available in a variety of sizes. This brush is recommended for use with the dry-brush stencil cremes. Note: The soft bristles and dome-shaped head of this brush may be preferred over the stiff, flat head of the stencil brush.

Makeup Sponge: This sponge has many tiny holes and a smooth surface that results in a velvety application of paint. A makeup sponge is inexpensive and can be discarded after use. For beginners, the most difficult obstacle to overcome is seeping. The most common cause of seeping is too much paint on the applicator. Because a makeup sponge is so dense, not a lot of paint can penetrate into it. Less paint on the applicator eliminates seeping.

Natural Sponge: This sea sponge has many holes of different shapes and sizes. This creates great texture and is perfect for stencilling objects that might naturally have this texture, such as a brick design.

Sponge Dauber: This applicator is shaped much like a thimble with a sponge attached to the tip of it. Placed on the index finger, it allows for great control of the paint application. The sponge on the dauber is made from the same material as a makeup sponge, so seeping is minimal.

Sponge Pouncer: This applicator has a stencilling sponge attached to a short wooden handle that fits comfortably in your hand. A sponge pouncer can be used with stencil creme, acrylic paint, and stencil gel. As with the makeup sponge and sponge dauber, the dense sponge eliminates most seeping.

Stencil Roller: This applicator is commonly made from foam and has tapered edges that prevent paint ridges. A roller is great for filling in large areas such as backgrounds or long strip borders.

For the best results, use a different sponge or brush for each color of paint that is used. This will eliminate the chance of "muddy" colors. Use smaller brushes for smaller stencil openings and larger brushes for larger stencil openings. This will save time and avoid frustration that comes with unwanted paint in the wrong area.

Using Tape

Stencil tape or low-tack masking tape is essential to successful stencilling. It will hold a tight edge to stencil against, but can be easily removed without lifting the paint or finish onto which it is taped. Here are a few of the common ways to use tape when stencilling:

1. Place small pieces of tape at the corners of the stencil to hold it in place while stencilling a basic design. This will enable you to have both hands free to work. Note: To hold more intricate stencils in place, stencil spray adhesive is recommended.

2. Tape off unwanted stencil openings. For example, the stencil design of a flower has a leaf. To stencil the flower without the leaf, cover the stencil opening for the unwanted leaf with the tape.

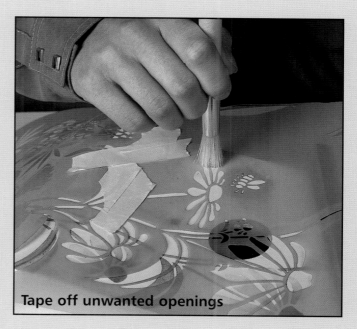

Tape off unwanted openings

3. Similarly, some stencil designs contain words. In some circumstances, such as when mirroring a design, the words may not be needed. To avoid words that are backward because the stencil has been flipped, tape off the words.

4. On some stencils, the design is cut too close to the edge, making it difficult to keep from painting over the stencil. Tape the edge to be safe. Prevent the possible mistake before it happens.

5. Tape off portions of a basic design stencil to create new designs. For example, taping off the lower portion of the medallion stencil will produce a new design that could be used to stencil a border to complement the original design on a particular project. This process also shortens the design and allows for fitting it into a smaller area.

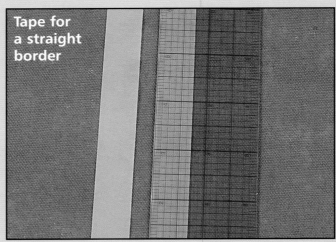

Tape for a straight border

Tape off to create new designs

Using Stencil Adhesives

Stencil adhesives are used to temporarily adhere the stencil onto the project. It is easily removed once the stencilling is complete and remains tacky for several applications. Although, in this book, the adhesive used is in the form of a spray, it is also available in a roll-on applicator.

Stencil Spray Adhesive: Spray adhesive is applied to the back of a stencil. A light coverage is sufficient to hold the stencil to the project. Allow the adhesive to dry for a few minutes until it becomes tacky before adhering it onto the project. This is recommended for almost any project because it forms a temporary bond especially around tiny stencil openings and eliminates "blurred" edges where the paint may have seeped under the stencil. Note: Spray adhesive is not recommended for mirrored designs.

6. Tape onto a surface to protect it from unwanted paint. This works well for tight corners, such as a wall border where the walls connect. Tape the adjacent wall to shield it when stencilling the other side.

7. Create a straight border by using a ruler to place two long pieces of tape, a determined width apart, along one edge of the project. Apply paint between the pieces of tape.

Stencil Spray Adhesive

Clean-up:
Mineral spirits and paper towels

Roll-on Applicator: Adhesive from a roll-on applicator is applied in only a few spots on the back of the stencil. This adhesive is used primarily to secure the stencil to the project and does not help avoid blurred edges. Once it is applied to the stencil, the drying time before adhering it onto the projects is 5–10 minutes.

General Stencilling Supplies
Baby oil
Brush basin and water
Disposable palettes
Matte acrylic spray
Paper towels
Pencil
Ruler
Stencil eraser

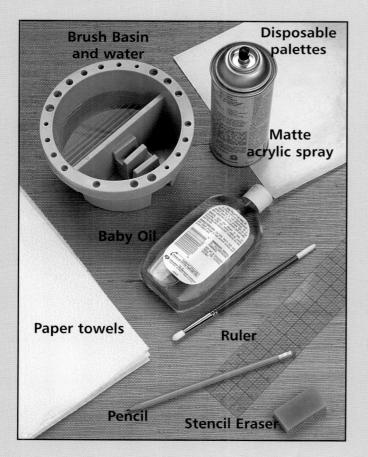

Brush Basin and water

Disposable palettes

Matte acrylic spray

Baby Oil

Paper towels

Ruler

Pencil

Stencil Eraser

Other Stencilling Supplies
Applicators: assorted flat brushes; sponge brushes
Butcher paper for mock-ups
Cardboard for stabilizing fabric
Craft scissors
Sandpaper
Self-adhesive notes

Organizing a Work Space
Make certain to have adequate space for completing the project. Keep the space free of clutter by setting out only the supplies needed for the project. Also, have plenty of paper towels on hand for easy clean-up.

Preparing Project Surfaces for Stencilling
Many surfaces require special preparation before applying the stencil design.

Preparing Unfinished Wood: Sand the wood. Using a tack cloth, remove all of the dust. Apply a clear wood sealer and allow to dry. Lightly sand and tack again.

Preparing Walls: Stencilling can be done on wallpaper, smooth walls, and textured walls. Make certain the surface is clean—free of dirt and oils—before beginning.

Paint plaster and drywall surfaces with two coats of a quality oil or latex wall paint that has a flat finish. Allow the paint to cure 24 hours before stencilling.

Flat or satin finish paints are preferred to semigloss paints which repel moisture. However, if the stencilling is to be done in an area such as a bathroom or kitchen where a semigloss finish is necessary due to frequent scrubbing, first lightly spray the area to be stencilled with a matte sealer. If a glossy wall finish is desired, paint the surface with a latex wall paint with a flat finish; do all stencilling, then cover the entire surface with a water-based urethane.

Preparing Fabric: Prewash and dry new fabric to remove the sizing. This will allow the paint to adhere better to the fabric. After the stencilling is complete, allow to dry 48 hours before any sewing or washing is done. Spot cleaning or hand-washing is recommended for cleaning stencilled fabric items.

Preparing Glassware: Clean the surface you will be painting with a vinegar and water mixture. Allow to dry before painting.

Preparing Tin: Wash the tin with vinegar to remove any oil. Allow to dry. Prime with tin primer. Allow the primer to cure 24 hours.

Preparing Concrete: Make certain the surface temperature of the concrete is above 50° F. Clean the concrete by scrubbing it with rubbing alcohol. Allow to dry.

Base-coating

This is the technique of applying several thin coats of paint to cover the project to create the "ground" for stencilling. Either a sponge brush or a large flat brush is most effective for this type of paint application as base-coating is generally used to cover large areas.

Base-coating

Backgrounds

A background can add dimension and texture to the effect of a stencilled design. However, too much background can overpower the stencilled design, causing it to appear messy or busy. Select a color that is slightly darker than the original ground color and apply it to the ground, using one or more of the following tools:

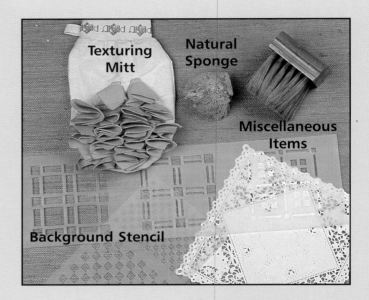

Texturing Mitt · Natural Sponge · Miscellaneous Items · Background Stencil

Natural Sponge: A natural sponge creates a soft look without definite lines. The sponge is moistened and then dried out on a paper towel. A very small amount of paint loaded and swirled onto the sponge goes a long way when randomly pounced over the surface of the ground.

Texturing Mitt: This is a cotton canvas mitten that has a texturing device such as a fabricated sponge, a natural sponge, mop strings, or rolled fabric sewn onto the palm. A mitt works best with glaze, which has a slower drying time and therefore allows for manipulating the paint to achieve the desired texture.

Background Stencil: There are an array of stencils that are specifically designed for producing backgrounds. A background stencil creates wonderful patterns that are more defined than those produced by a sponge or a texturing mitt. Take care when selecting the design and the paint color to choose something that does not distract from the main stencilling.

Miscellaneous Items: Some items such as a paper doily naturally double as stencils. Refer to "Angels Among Us" Scrapbook Page on page 45. Before placing it onto the project surface, carefully look over the doily for any openings that may contain loose paper that did not release when manufactured. Use a needle or sharp point to pop out these tiny pieces of paper. Because the doily is difficult to handle when it is moist, avoid using spray adhesive to adhere it onto the project surface. Hold the doily in place and, using a makeup sponge, apply paint into the openings of the doily. This creates a great background texture.

Try using stiff brushes, wadded pieces of fabric, paper, or cellophane to achieve background effects similar to those produced with the texturing mitts.

Stencilling Order

Stencilling has an order for completing each project. It is a simple and clean craft to master.

1. Position the stencil on the project as desired.

2. Tape the stencil onto the project or spray the back side of the stencil with stencil spray adhesive and then adhere it onto the project.

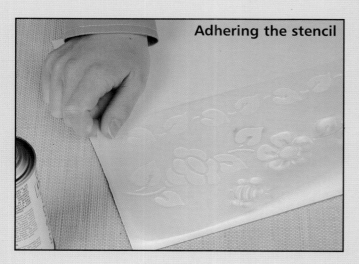

Adhering the stencil

3. Use a "dry-brush" technique to load the applicator and apply the paint.

a. Loading the Applicator

This is by far the most important part of stencilling and the step that can either take the credit for successful stencilling or the blame for less successful stencilling. The goal of stencilling is to produce clean, crisp lines. Achieving this goal begins with the amount of paint loaded onto the applicator before the stencilling process even begins. The best way to describe how much paint to use is by saying "less is better." It is far easier to add more paint than it is to correct too much paint. This rule applies to all paints and cremes.

- Holding the applicator upright, lightly dip it into a small amount of paint.
- Work the paint into the applicator by lightly rubbing it in a circular motion on a disposable palette.

Working the paint into the applicator

23

- Remove excess paint from the applicator by lightly rubbing it in a circular motion on a paper towel until it appears to be dry.

Removing excess paint on a paper towel

b. Stroke

A stroke is the brush technique used to apply paint through the openings of the stencil. There are three basic strokes—circular, pouncing, and sweeping. Some strokes work better for certain types of paint. For example, the pouncing stroke is recommended with air-dry enamel paints because it works better with the paint's consistency. However, when deciding on which stroke to use, one is not necessarily more correct than the other—it is largely a matter of preference. Whichever you choose per project, it is important to be consistent and continue with the same stroke until the project is completed.

- Hold the applicator perpendicular to the surface of the project.
- Using either a circular, pouncing, or sweeping motion, lightly apply the paints into the openings of the stencil. Repeat if necessary for a more solid application.

Circular Stroke: This stroke moves in a circular pattern from the outside edge of the stencil opening to the inside. Naturally, the paint application is heavier or darker at the outside edge and becomes lighter toward the center as less paint remains in the applicator, creating a highlight and resulting in a striking visual effect. This stroke works best when combined with stencil brushes and stencil cremes.

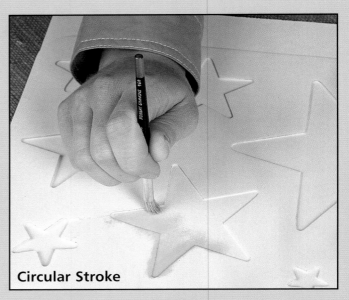

Circular Stroke

The circular stroke is not recommended for use with acrylic paints or air-dry enamels. Also, avoid using any sort of sponge as an applicator. Since the consistency of stencil creme is so thick and because the sponge is difficult to swirl, combining either of these two with the circular stroke will almost certainly result in paint seeping under the stencil.

Pouncing Stroke: A makeup sponge or sponge pouncer works best for the pouncing stroke. With this stroke, the paint is applied in an up-and-down motion. This stroke also yields a highlight effect, but unlike the circular stroke, the application begins in the center of the stencil opening and works toward the outside edge. A light pounce results in light coverage. The heavier the pounce, the more solid the application. This simple stroke is good for beginners as seeping is less likely to occur.

24

Note: This stroke is recommended over the others because it results in fewer mistakes.

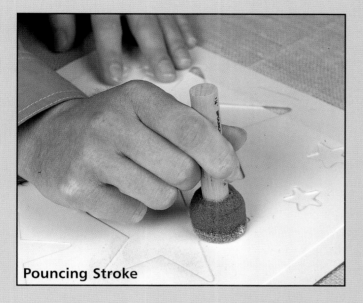

Pouncing Stroke

Sweeping Stroke: This stroke, which also works best with a makeup sponge or sponge pouncer, moves in a back-and-forth motion and gives a definite direction to the paint application. This stroke is very effective for basing in the color of large areas. First apply the paint with the sweeping stroke and then go back over it with another stroke.

Sweeping Stroke

4. When stencilling is complete, carefully lift and remove the stencil. Allow to dry.

Highlighting & Shading

Selecting paint colors and determining the order in which they are applied depends on whether the highlighting or shading is done with the same color or if it is done with another color. The best rule to remember when highlighting and shading is to apply the colors from the lightest paint colors to the darkest paint colors. Even when highlighting with the same color, it is easiest to stencil a darker color over a lighter color than it is vice versa.

Highlighting With the Same Color: This technique is achieved by using the circular stroke when applying color. Begin with the heaviest amount of paint first at the stencil opening edge; work all around the edge and gradually move toward the center. The amount of paint on the applicator decreases and the result is a highlight effect.

Highlighting With the Same Color

Shading (Highlighting With Another Color): This technique successfully blends two complementary colors—one for the undertone and one for the shading. The rule is to apply dark over light. For example, for stencilling a star, light blue is chosen for the highlight color and purple is chosen for the shading color. Because light blue is lighter in color, it is applied first. Using the circular stroke, begin with the heaviest amount of paint first at the stencil opening edge; work all around the edge and gradually move toward the center. The purple is then applied over the light blue. Using the pouncing stroke to avoid smearing the two colors, lightly apply purple along the edges of the star where the shadows would be.

Shading (Highlighting With Another Color)

Repeating the Design for Length

There are two methods for determining whether a repeating design will fit within the length of the project. The first is the continuous technique and the second is the centered technique. Which to use depends on the style of stencil you have chosen.

Continuous Technique: This is usually used when the design elements are small and the design flows in one direction. Begin stencilling at one end and continue around the project, repeating the design approximately two-thirds the total length. Determine whether the stencil design needs to be adjusted to fit before reaching the other end. Adjust the stencil design by stretching, squeezing, or adding to the design. Note: It is helpful to make a paper mock-up to determine which technique will best solve the problem.

Continuous Technique

Centered Technique: This technique is generally used when the design has a large element in the center and gradually gets smaller at both ends. Position the design at the center of the project length and begin stencilling. Continue, repeating the design at the left and right of the first stencilled design. As for continuous stencilling, stop before reaching the end of the project and adjust the stencil design to fit the available space by stretching, squeezing, or adding to the design.

Centered Technique

designed by Melanie Royals © 1999 Photo by Alain Auzanneau

Stretching the Design: To ease the design so it fits on the project, increase the space between design motifs approximately ½"–1" per repeat. This means that for every five elements of the design, there should be approximately ⅛"–³⁄₁₆" more space between each element. This minor adjustment will not be as noticeable as an area at the end of the project length that is not large enough to fit the entire design.

Stretching the Design

Squeezing the Design: This is using the same principles as stretching the design, but subtracting instead of adding space. Place the elements of the design closer together to ease into the available space.

Squeezing the Design

Adding to the Design: This technique can be used with a continuous border that contains motifs that can stand alone, such as these fishing tackle pieces. These motifs can be added onto a completed stencil design to extend the design in a natural-looking way. This technique comes in handy for easing into corners and filling in areas too small to accommodate an entire repeat.

Some stencilling kits even offer an extra stencil or two with individual motifs for this purpose.

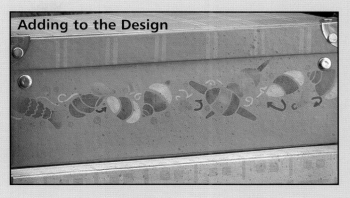

Adding to the Design

Clean-up & Caring for Stencils & Applicators

When the stencilling project is complete, clean the applicators with soap and water. For brushes, try to find soap in a container that has a bristle scrubber built into the lid. Work the paint out of the bristles on the scrubber. Rinse clean with running water. Never soak a stencil brush in water. Blot the brush on a paper towel to remove excess water. Even brushes that may have been used in oil-based stencil cremes are easy to clean this way.

Place all brushes on their sides to dry. For larger brushes, loop a rubber band around the bristles and roll it to the ends of the bristles to keep bristles from splaying. Store dry brushes flat or on their handle ends with the bristles up. Brushes should be completely dry before they are used again.

Use baby oil to clean the stencils. Take care when removing the paint. Pay attention to any small section of the stencil that may lift up or bend. Work on a flat surface with a paper towel under the stencil. Rub the stencil gently with the baby oil and then rinse it with water. Place the stencil between two paper towels and press lightly to remove the moisture. Store the stencil in a large box that is big enough to allow the stencil to lay flat.

Section 2: *techniques*

How do I accomplish basic stencilling using a single overlay stencil?

What You Need to Get Started:

Acrylic paints:
  dark golden
  yellow; light
  golden yellow
Applicators:
  makeup sponges;
  sponge brushes
Disposable palette
Matte acrylic spray
Paper towels
Sandpaper
Scrapbooking
  templates:
  geometric shapes
Stencil spray
  adhesive
Wooden box

This stencil is actually a template made for scrapbooking. Templates double quite nicely as stencils. The way the template is used here is known as "single overlay stencilling" because only one stencil is required to complete the design.

Geo Shapes Box

Here's How:
1. Refer to Preparing Unfinished Wood on page 21. Prepare the wood.

2. Refer to Base-coating on page 22. Using a sponge brush, base-coat box with light golden yellow.

3. Using a sponge brush, base-coat lid with dark golden yellow.

4. Spray the back side of stencil with spray adhesive. Adhere stencil onto one side of box, making certain some shapes extend beyond the edge and wrap around corners.

5. Refer to Stencilling Order on pages 23–24. Using makeup sponges, apply dark golden yellow paint into the openings of stencils. Remove stencil and allow to dry.

6. Repeat Steps 4 and 5 for each remaining side.

7. Tape stencils onto lid, making certain to line up shapes that extended

from the edge of box and wrap from sides to top.

8. Using makeup sponges, apply light golden yellow paint into the openings of stencils. Remove stencil and allow to dry.

9. Using sandpaper, sand along the edges of box and lid.

10. Spray box with matte acrylic spray.

2 technique

How do I use more than one paint color with a bridged stencil?

What You Need to Get Started:

Acrylic paints:
  black; blue; light
  blue; green;
  ivory; pink; tan;
  white; yellow
Applicators: #3
  liner brush;
  makeup sponges;
  sponge brushes
Disposable palette
Matte acrylic spray
Paper towels
Sandpaper
Stencil: bee and
  flowers
Stencil spray
  adhesive
Wooden box

This project is perfect for the beginner. Find a simple bridged stencil that looks easy and has only a few design elements.

Bees & Posies Box

Here's How:

1. Refer to Preparing Unfinished Wood Surfaces on page 21. Prepare the wood.

2. Refer to Base-coating on page 22. Using a sponge brush, base-coat lid of box with light blue paint. Allow to dry.

3. Using a sponge brush, base-coat body of box with ivory paint. Allow to dry.

4. Using sandpaper, sand along the edges of box.

5. Spray the back side of stencil with spray adhesive. Adhere stencil on-to box.

6

6. Refer to Stencilling Order on pages 23–24. Using makeup sponges, apply paint into the openings of stencil. Re-peat the design if necessary. Remove stencil and allow to dry.

7. Repeat the bee motif around box and on lid. Remove stencil and allow to dry.

8. Using liner brush, paint "stitch" marks with white paint for a trail be-hind bees.

9. Spray box with matte acrylic spray.

Tips:

Use tape to mask off the openings of unwanted motifs.

Use a small amount of paint when

stencilling. Repeat the color application in the openings to achieve a solid effect.

Troubleshooting:

Avoid loading too much paint onto the sponge or brush. Too little is far better than too much. Repeating color is easier than trying to fix paint that has seeped under the stencil.

Measure both the stencil and the wooden box before painting to ensure the proper placement of motifs.

3
technique

What You Need to Get Started:

Acrylic paints: green; light green; dark red; red; golden yellow; light golden yellow
Antiquing spray
Applicators: makeup sponges; natural sponge; sponge brushes
Disposable palette
Matte acrylic spray
Paper towels
Sandpaper
Stencil: ½" checkerboard
Stencil spray adhesive
Wooden boxes (3)

How do I accomplish basic stencilling with a textured ground?

As simple as this project is to create, the end result is very satisfying. Texturing and using the most basic stencil can add character to an otherwise ordinary item.

Checkered Boxes

Here's How:

1. Refer to Preparing Unfinished Wood on page 21. Prepare the wood.

2. Refer to Base-coating on page 22. Using a sponge brush, base-coat box and lid with one dark color.

3. Mix coordinating light color with dark color used for base coat in a 1:4 ratio. Note: The result will be a slightly lighter color than the base-coat color.

4. Dampen natural sponge with water. Remove all excess water from sponge on a paper towel. Dip sponge into mixed paint, swirl sponge onto palette to distribute paint across sponge, and lightly pounce over the surface of box and lid to create texture. Allow to dry.

5. Spray the back side of stencil with spray adhesive. Adhere stencil onto textured box.

6. Add a small amount of light color into previously mixed paint for a lighter color.

7. Refer to Stencilling Order on pages 23–24. Using makeup sponges, apply paint into the openings of stencil. Move stencil and repeat the design to cover box and lid. Remove stencil and allow to dry.

7

Troubleshooting:

When mixing the paints to achieve lighter shades, make certain to mix enough. Nothing is worse than running out of a mixed paint in the middle of a project—and then trying to mix and match to the color already on the project.

If your project has a lid and if the stencil is being repeated from the lid to the main area, keep the lid on when texturing and stencilling. The motifs will line up and it makes completing the project much faster.

8. Using sandpaper, sand along the edges of box and lid.

9. Carefully mist the edges of box with antiquing spray.

10. Spray box with matte acrylic spray.

11. Repeat Steps 1 through 9 for each remaining box.

Tips:

A slight variance in color is better than a harsh difference when texturing. It is always better to add small amounts of the contrasting color and gradually get lighter.

If the project has a handle or knob, see if it is removable before beginning the project. It will save a lot of time that might be wasted on trying to stencil around a knob.

Practice using the antiquing spray as it is not easy to correct.

How do I use stencils with registration marks?

What You Need to Get Started:

Applicators: 1½"
  flat brush;
  makeup sponges;
  natural sponge
Butcher paper:
  32" square
Canvas: 32" square
Craft knife
Disposable palette
Fabric scissors
Glazing paint:
  off-white
Indoor/outdoor
  paint: blue
Latex wall paint:
  off-white
Masking tape:
  ¾" wide
Matte acrylic spray
Paper towels
Pencil
Ruler
Self-adhesive notes
Stencil roller: small
Stencil spray
  adhesive
Stencil set:
  medallion and
  scroll

Some stencil designs require using registration marks to line them up and ensure accurate placement on the project. They are relatively easy to use and save time that might otherwise be wasted on fixing mistakes because designs are placed incorrectly.

Medallion Floor Mat

Here's How:

1. Using stencils and pencil, make a mock-up of floor mat design on a piece of butcher paper to ensure placement of stencils. Transfer all registration marks. Place mock-up nearby for easy reference.

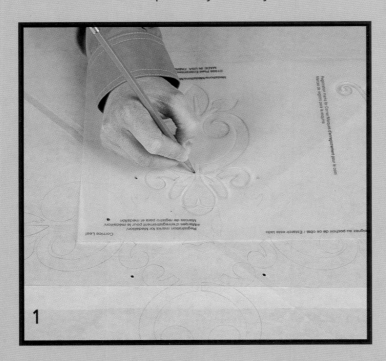

2. Using flat brush, paint canvas with wall paint to stiffen canvas. Allow to dry for 24 hours.

3. Refer to Base-coating on page 22. Using flat brush, base-coat canvas with indoor/outdoor paint. Allow to dry.

4. Mix indoor/outdoor paint and glazing paint in a 2:1 ratio on disposable palette.

5. Dampen natural sponge with water. Remove all excess water from sponge on a paper towel. Dip sponge into mixed paint, swirl sponge onto palette to distribute paint across sponge, and lightly pounce over the surface of canvas to create texture. Allow to dry.

6. Using pencil, trace the outside line of mat onto canvas.

7. Using pencil and self-adhesive notes, transfer all registration marks onto canvas. Note: The self-

adhesive notes are easily removed once the stencilling is complete and will not harm or mar the canvas mat.

8. Spray the back side of stencils with spray adhesive. Adhere stencils onto canvas, making certain all registration marks line up.

9. Refer to Stencilling Order on pages 23–24. Using makeup sponges, apply glazing paint into the openings for center motif first.

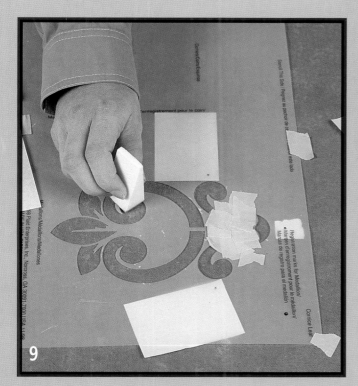

10. Apply paint into the openings for the outside edge motifs, beginning with corners.

11. Once corners are stencilled, apply paint into the openings for the center border motifs.

12. Carefully remove stencils without disturbing registration marks.

13. Using ruler, place two long pieces of masking tape ¼" apart, along each side of mat, and

centered within stencilled motifs. Using craft knife and taking care not to cut canvas, square tape corners.

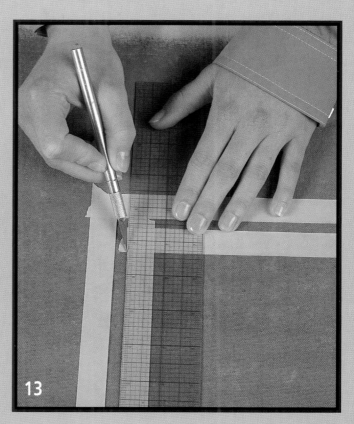

14. Using stencil roller, apply mixed paint between tape strips to create border. Allow to dry 24–48 hours and remove tape.

15. Using ruler, place two long pieces of masking tape ⅜" apart along the edge of each side of canvas. Using craft knife, square corners.

16. Using stencil roller, apply mixed paint between tape strips to create border. Allow to dry 24–48 hours and remove tape.

17. Spray canvas several times with matte acrylic spray.

18. Using fabric scissors, cut canvas along the outside line.

How do I use other objects as stencils?

Stencils can be made from almost anything. Any object that can produce a nice clean edge can be regarded as a stencil. This project should provide ideas for what can be used as a stencil.

Outdoor Frame

Here's How:

1. Using cotton cloth, evenly apply wood stain over the surface of frame. Allow to dry.

2. On cutting mat, place tin tree on one piece of card stock, allowing ¼" all around.

3. Using craft knife, cut card stock around tree.

4. Repeat Steps 1 and 2 for tin stars.

5. Using wave decorative-edged scissors, cut along one long edge of remaining piece of card stock. Using deckle decorative-edged scissors, cut along remaining long edge of card stock.

6. For trees in the background, position card stock tree stencil high on one side of frame.

7. Refer to Stencilling Order on pages 23–24. Using a makeup sponge, apply stain into the opening of stencil. Remove stencil and allow to dry.

What You Need to Get Started:

Applicators:
  makeup sponges
Card stock:
  8½" x 11" (2)
Cotton cloth
Craft knife
Cutting mat
Decorative-edged
  scissors: deckle;
  wave
Disposable palette
Hammer
Matte acrylic spray
Paper towels
Tack nails (6)
Tin shapes: bear;
  fish; moon;
  medium star;
  small star; large
  tree
Wood stain
Wooden frame:
  unfinished

5

6–7

39

8. For trees that appear to be closer, reposition stencil lower on frame. Repeat Step 7 without removing stencil. Repeat Step 7 again for a darker image. Remove stencil and allow to dry. Continue in this manner, moving stencil lower and applying additional layers of stain until completing a dark tree in the foreground.

9. Repeat Steps 6 through 8 on the remaining side of frame.

10. Position star stencils on the upper section of frame. Repeat Step 7 for stars.

11. Position tin moon on the upper corner of frame. Using makeup sponge, apply stain in an outward motion from the edges of moon onto frame. Allow to dry.

12. Place the deckle edge of card stock pointing downward at base of trees on frame.

13. Using makeup sponge, apply stain in a downward motion from the edge of card stock onto frame. Move the card stock edge and repeat as desired. Allow to dry.

14. Place the wave edge of card stock pointing upward on the bottom section of frame.

15. Apply stain in an upward motion from the edge of card stock to frame. Move the card stock edge down and to one side and repeat. Continue in this manner to fill section. Allow to dry.

16. Spray frame with matte acrylic spray.

17. Using hammer and tack nails, attach tin shapes to frame as desired.

Tips:

Predrill the tin shapes before attaching them to the frame. The hole makes it easier to hammer the tack nail into the frame.

Troubleshooting:

Avoid applying too much stain. Begin with a light application and repeat for a darker motif.

How do I add shading to the stencilling?

Shading is the most rewarding technique in stencilling. It is much easier than it looks. Do not be afraid to paint a leaf with three to four colors—there really are that many colors in an actual leaf. Shading adds dimension and depth to the project, making it look as if it were done by a professional.

Fruit Drawers

Here's How:
1. Refer to Preparing Unfinished Wood on page 21. Prepare the wood.

2. Apply wood stain over the entire surface of chest. Allow to dry 6–8 hours.

3. Remove drawer knobs. Using flat brush, apply green paint to knobs, chest base, and chest top.

4. Refer to Base-coating on page 22. Using flat brush, base-coat drawer fronts with ivory paint.

5. One drawer at a time, position stencil as desired for varied images.

6. Spray the back side of stencil with spray adhesive. Adhere stencil onto drawer front.

7. Refer to Stencilling Order on pages 23–24. Using stencil brushes, apply stencil creme, beginning with the lightest shade and working toward the darkest, into the openings of stencil. Remove stencil and allow to dry.

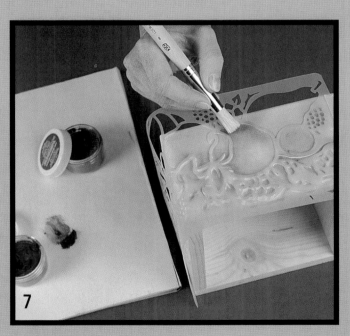

7

8. Spray each stencilled drawer with matte acrylic spray. Allow to dry.

9. Reattach drawer knobs.

What You Need to Get Started:

Acrylic paints: dark green; ivory
Antiquing spray
Applicators:
  1½" flat brush;
  stencil brushes
Chest of drawers:
  small
Disposable palette
Matte acrylic spray
Paper towels
Stencil: fruits
Stencil cremes:
  blue; dark
  brown; reddish
  brown; dark
  green; green;
  dark red; purple;
  reddish purple;
  golden yellow;
  sunflower yellow
Stencil spray
  adhesive
Wood stain

10. Carefully mist edges of each drawer with antiquing spray. Allow to dry.

11. Spray chest with several coats of matte acrylic spray. Allow to dry between coats.

How do I use ink pads with stencils?

The materials for this project are easy to acquire—especially if you already have ink pads for rubber stamping. Ink pads, available in a single color or with 10–12 colors on one pad, make stencilling on paper quick and convenient.

What You Need to Get Started:

Applicators: sponge daubers
Cards and envelopes: premade
Disposable palette
Embossing template: assorted greetings
Embossing stylus
Light table
Paper towels
Pigment ink pads: assorted colors
Stencil: flowers
Stencil spray adhesive
Stencil tape

Handmade Greeting Cards

Here's How:

1. Spray the back side of stencil with spray adhesive. Adhere stencil onto card.

2. Refer to Stencilling Order on pages 23–24. Using sponge daubers, apply ink, beginning with the lightest color and working toward the darkest, into the openings of stencil. Remove stencil and allow to dry.

3. Repeat Step 2 for a partial motif on envelope.

4. Position embossing template on the front of card in an area that has not been stencilled. Tape template in place.

5. Open card and turn it over so card is on top of template. Place card and template on light table. Using stylus, gently press card through the openings of template, creating a raised design. Remove tape and template.

Tips:

A small amount of ink goes a long way. If some of the openings of the stencils are tiny,

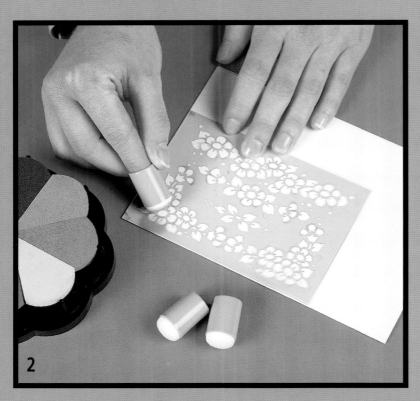

2

try using a cotton swab as an applicator.

Daub very lightly when stencilling with the pigment ink.

Since the colors are so strong, do not hesitate to mix the colors. A little brown ink stencilled over bright yellow will tone it right down.

Troubleshooting:

Avoid pressing the sponge daubers too hard into the ink pad. Make certain to remove excess ink from daubers onto paper towels, as too much ink will seep under the stencil.

Make certain the ink is dry before embossing to avoid any smearing.

How do I cut my own stencil?

Cutting your own stencil allows more freedom when determining the area that will be stencilled. Self-cut designs can range from quite simple to quite intricate. However, this technique does require a certain amount of patience and practice.

"Angels Among Us" Scrapbook Page

Here's How:

1. Place drawing or picture on work surface. If desired, use Grapevine Drawings and Grapevine Cutting Patterns on pages 48–49.

2. Tape tracing paper onto the top of drawing or picture.

3. Using pencil, trace one element of drawing or picture.

4. Remove tape, move tracing paper at least ½", and repeat Step 2.

5. Repeat Steps 3 and 4 until all elements have been individually traced.

6. Place stencil blank right side up on work surface. Tape tracing paper onto stencil blank.

7. Turn stencil blank over so tracing paper is now on work surface with the traced designs showing through.

8. Using permanent marker, trace designs onto the back side of stencil blank.

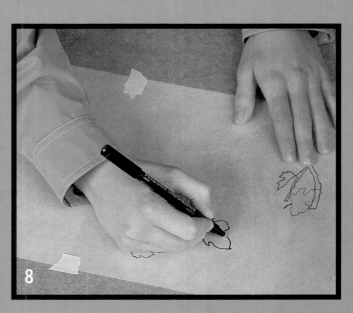

9. Turn stencil blank over again and remove tracing paper.

What You Need to Get Started:

Acrylic paints: brown; ivory
Adhesive: acid-free
Applicators: #3 liner brush; makeup sponges
Brush marker: black
Card stock: dark green, 12" x 12"; light green, 8½" x 11"; ivory, 11" x 11"; speckled ivory, 8½" x 11"; plum, 8½" x 11"; light tan, 8½" x 11"
Craft knife
Craft scissors
Drawing or picture
Glass cutting mat
Matte acrylic spray
Paper doily: 8"
Paper towel
Pencil
Permanent marker: fine-point
Photo corners: embossed, ivory (8); laser-cut, small, ivory (8)
Photographs
Stencil blank
Stencil cremes: colonial blue; brown; dark brown; olive green; lavender; reddish purple; golden yellow
Stencil tape
Swivel knife
Tracing paper

10. Place stencil blank on cutting mat. Using craft knife for straight lines and swivel knife for curves, carefully cut out the traced designs.

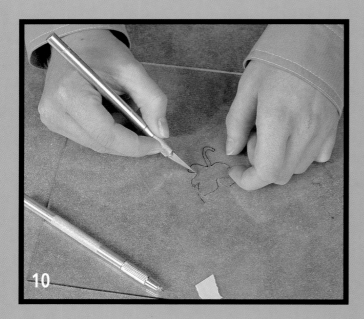

11. Center doily onto ivory card stock for a stencil.

12. Refer to Stencilling Order on pages 23–24. Holding doily in place and using makeup sponges, apply thinned ivory paint into the openings of doily, beginning in the center, working toward the outer edge, then fading out about ½" beyond the doily edge. Remove doily and allow to dry.

13. Tape stencil onto card stock, placing the first element such as the branch as desired.

14. Using makeup sponges or stencil brushes, apply stencil cremes into the openings of stencil. Remove stencil and allow to dry.

15. Remove tape, move stencil so the next element such as the grape builds upon the first. Repeat Step 14. Continue in this manner until the design is complete.

16. Using liner brush, paint other embellishments such as the veins on the leaves and the tendrils on the grapevine as desired.

17. Carefully mist stencilled areas with matte acrylic spray.

18. Using acid-free adhesive, adhere stencilled card stock onto the center of dark green card stock.

19. Adhere each photograph onto speckled ivory card stock. Using craft scissors, cut card stock ⅛" larger all around than photograph.

20. Adhere photographs again onto colored card stock. For smaller photographs, cut card stock ¼" larger all around than speckled ivory card stock. For larger photographs, cut card stock ⅜" larger all around than speckled ivory card stock.

21. Adhere the photo corners onto each photograph.

22. Arrange photographs and mount them as desired onto stencilled card stock.

23. Using brush marker, add lettering as desired.

Tips:
Choose a very simple design. Fabric patterns make wonderful stencils. Coordinate designs to decorate a room from the bedspread to pillows to the wall border.

When cutting the stencil blank, always pull the blade toward you, turning the cutting surface. Clean-cut lines make the best stencils.

Mylar sheets and card stock are also good materials for creating stencils.

Try using an electric stencil cutter.

Troubleshooting:
Practice. It is the only way to get control of the knives.

Avoid jagged lines. Long continuous lines are the best.

Grapevine Drawings

Grapevine B

Grapevine A

Grapevine C

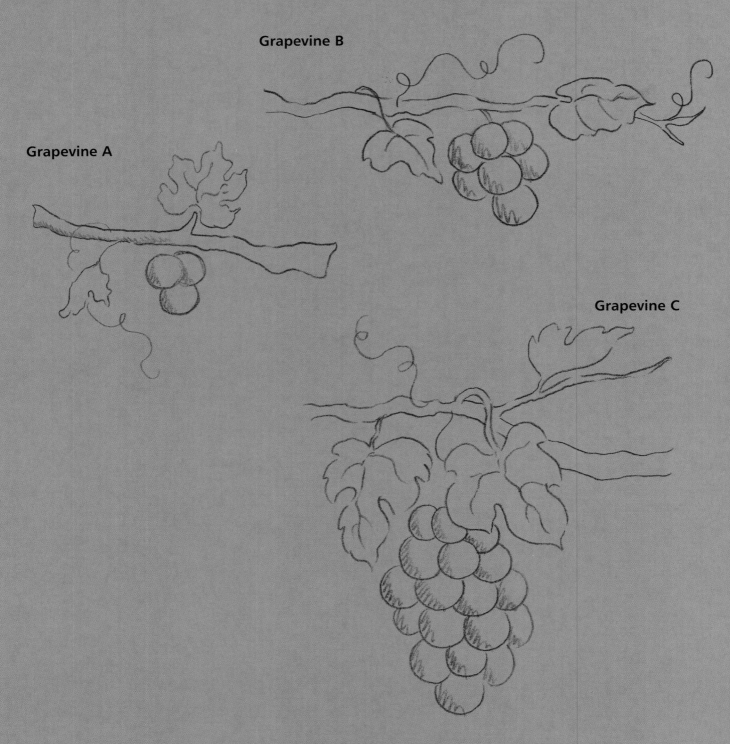

Grapevine Cutting Patterns

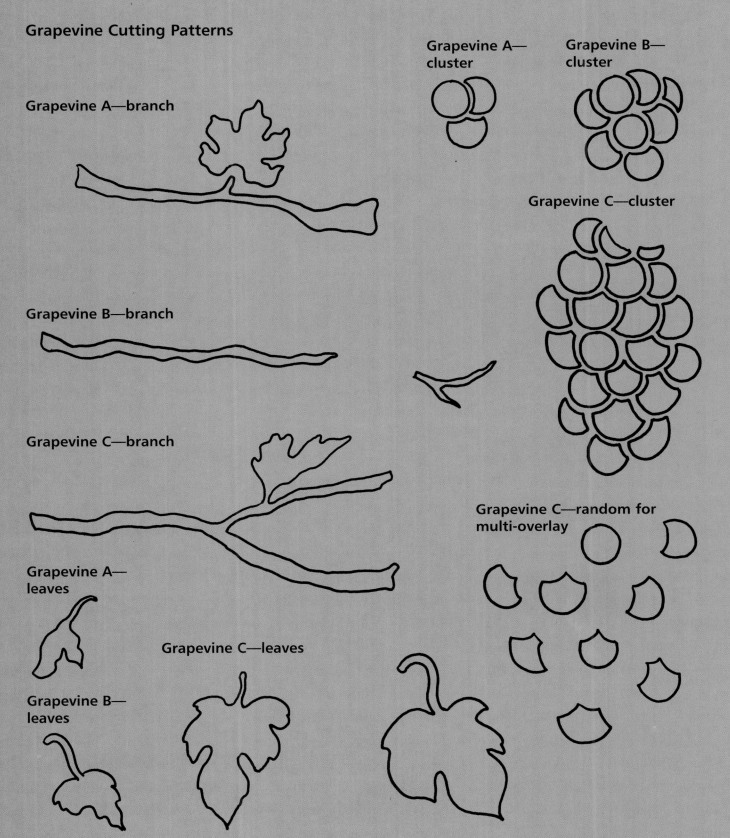

Grapevine A—cluster

Grapevine B—cluster

Grapevine A—branch

Grapevine C—cluster

Grapevine B—branch

Grapevine C—branch

Grapevine C—random for multi-overlay

Grapevine A—leaves

Grapevine C—leaves

Grapevine B—leaves

49

How do I create plaid effects using a stencil?

Acrylic paints:
black; blue; dark brown; golden brown; light brown; dark olive green; light olive green; light sage green; ivory; dark off-white; orange; rustic red; golden yellow
Antiquing spray
Applicators:
makeup sponges; sponge brushes
Disposable palette
Paper towels
Matte acrylic spray
Nested boxes (3)
Stencil tape
Stencils: cabin; fishing; plaids

Different plaid designs look great in coordinating colors and also work well as backgrounds for tying similar themed motifs together.

Fishing Boxes

Here's How:

1. Refer to Base-coating on page 22. Using a sponge brush, base-coat body of small box and lid of large box with light brown paint. Allow to dry.

2. Using a sponge brush, base-coat body of medium box and lid of small box with light sage green paint. Allow to dry.

3. Using a sponge brush, base-coat body of large box and lid of medium box with ivory paint. Allow to dry.

4. Tape one plaid stencil onto lid of large box.

5. Mix a very small amount of ivory paint with light brown paint. Refer to Stencilling Order on pages 23–24. Using makeup sponges, apply mixed paint into the openings of stencil. Remove stencil and allow to dry.

6. Tape a different plaid stencil onto lid of medium box.

7. Using makeup sponges, apply dark off-white paint into the openings of

stencil. Remove stencil and allow to dry.

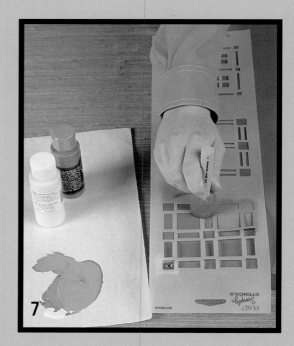

8. Tape a different plaid stencil onto lid of small box.

9. Mix a very small amount of ivory paint with light sage green paint. Using makeup sponges, apply mixed paint into the openings of stencil. Remove stencil and allow to dry.

10. Tape cabin and fishing stencils onto body of each box.

11. Using makeup sponges, apply assorted colors of paint, beginning with the lightest shade and working toward the darkest, into the openings of stencils. Remove stencils and allow to dry.

12. Spray each box and lid with matte acrylic spray. Allow to dry.

13. Carefully mist the edges of each box with antiquing spray. Allow to dry.

14. Repeat Step 12.

Tips:
When mixing the paints for the lids, add the lighter color slowly to avoid getting it too light. A subtle difference is best.

Always mix enough paint to avoid running out before the lids are completed.

Troubleshooting:
Avoid using stencilling cremes as they seem to create a halo effect on paper boxes.

Make certain the lid is on when placing the stencil on the body of the box to know how far down to position it.

Make certain the matte spray and antiquing spray are allowed to dry between layers to avoid "running."

How can I alter the design of my stencil?

Sometimes a stencil may have a motif that you would like to use, but the entire design does not fit your project. By taping off unwanted motifs and repositioning the stencil during the process of paint application, you can create your own design.

What You Need to Get Started:

Acrylic paints:
  dark brown;
  light brown;
  ivory
Applicators:
  sponge brushes;
  stencil brushes
Disposable palette
Matte acrylic spray
Paper towels
Stencil cremes:
  brownish black;
  light blue;
  reddish brown;
  olive green;
  golden yellow;
  sunflower yellow
Stencil spray
  adhesive
Stencil tape
Stencils:
  wildflower
  border; wood-
  grain
Wooden birdhouse

Sunflower Birdhouse

Here's How:

1. Refer to Preparing Unfinished Wood on page 21. Prepare the wood.

2. Refer to Base-coating on page 22. Using a sponge brush, base-coat roof of birdhouse with light brown paint. Allow to dry.

3. Using a sponge brush, base-coat body of birdhouse with ivory paint. Allow to dry.

4. Spray the back side of wood-grain stencil with spray adhesive. Adhere stencil onto roof.

5. Refer to Stencilling Order on pages 23–24. Using stencil brushes, apply dark brown paint into the openings of stencil. Repeat the design if necessary. Remove stencil and allow to dry.

6. Spray the back side of wild-flower border stencil with spray adhesive. Position stencil as desired for the first image. Adhere stencil onto body of birdhouse. Tape off any unwanted motifs.

7. Using stencil brushes, apply stencil cremes, beginning with the lightest shade and working toward the darkest, into the openings of stencil. Remove stencil and allow to dry.

7

8. Carefully mist stencilled areas with matte acrylic spray. Allow to dry.

9. Reposition stencil for the next motif. Repeat Steps 7 and 8. Continue in this manner around body of birdhouse.

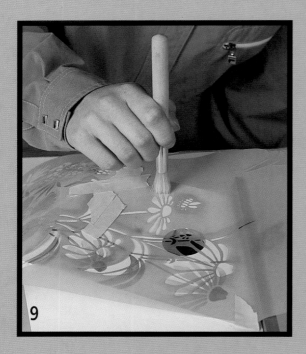

9

10. Spray entire birdhouse with matte acrylic spray.

Tips:

In areas that may have a "broken stem" resulting from taping off a flower, fill in the broken areas with a small image, such as a bee.

Altering the height of the same flower several times around the birdhouse causes it to look like a different flower. To create even more difference, add an extra leaf or a buzzing bee nearby.

Troubleshooting:

Lightly misting each stenciled area with matte acrylic spray helps avoid smearing between layers. This will also help keep the paint from sticking to the back of the next adhesive-sprayed stencil.

54

How do I mirror stencil designs?

When a space does not permit using the entire stencil design, use just a portion of it and then flip it over, creating a mirrored image and filling the space.

What You Need to Get Started:

Acrylic paints:
sage green; ivory
Applicators:
sponge brushes;
stencil brushes
Disposable palette
Matte acrylic spray
Paper towels
Sandpaper
Stencil: beehive
and garden
accents
Stencil cremes:
black; colonial
blue; grayish
brown; reddish
brown; olive
green; terra-
cotta orange;
pink; rusty red;
golden yellow;
sunflower yellow
Stencil tape
Tape measure
Wooden shelf
with removable
backer board

Beehive Shelf

Here's How:
1. Remove backer board from shelf.

2. Refer to Preparing Unfinished Wood on page 21. Prepare the wood.

3. Refer to Base-coating on page 22. Using a sponge brush, base-coat shelf with sage green paint. Allow to dry.

4. Using sandpaper, sand along the edges of shelf.

5. Using a sponge brush, base-coat backer board with ivory paint. Allow to dry.

6. Using tape measure, measure backer board. Measure stencil. Determine the portion of stencil to be used and flipped to accomplish a mirrored image that will fit on backer board. Allow for the edge which will be covered when backer board is reattached to shelf.

7. Tape stencil onto one side of backer board.

8. Refer to Stencilling Order on pages 23–24. Using stencil brushes, apply stencil cremes, beginning with the lightest shade and working toward the darkest, into the openings of stencil. Remove stencil and allow to dry.

9. Carefully mist stencilled areas with matte acrylic spray. Allow to dry.

10. Carefully clean stencil of any residual paint. Flip stencil over and tape it onto the blank side of backer board.

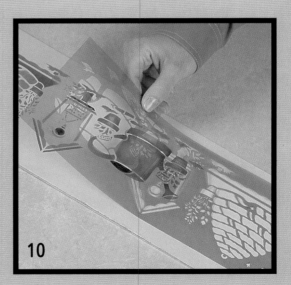

10

11. Repeat Step 8.

12. Spray backer board with matte acrylic spray.

13. Reattach backer board onto shelf.

14. Spray entire shelf with matte acrylic spray.

Tips:

Small images such as flowers can be added to fill a negative space that may have been created when the stencil was repeated.

Stencil cremes take longer to dry. To avoid any smearing, lightly mist the finished area with matte acrylic spray before stencilling the mirrored image.

Troubleshooting:

When using a stencil with lettering, tape off the letters to avoid reversing them in the process of stencilling the mirrored image. This lettering can be added later.

Tape off unwanted openings that overlap previously stencilled images. Be aware of where the desired image comes to an end and tape off any following openings. Pay close attention to where the images run close to the edge of the project.

How do I use component stencils?

The individual components that make up this design include flowers, flowerpots, a dirt mound, a spade, a bee, and fence posts. Using separate motifs allows the freedom of varied placement on the project, creating a unique scene.

What You Need to Get Started:

Acrylic paints:
  light blue;
  brown; ivory
Antiquing spray
Applicators: 1"
  flat brush;
  stencil brushes
Crackle medium
Disposable palette
Lamp kit
Lamp shade: 11"
Paper towels
Sandpaper
Stencil cremes:
  black; dark
  brown; light
  brown; reddish
  brown; colonial
  green; olive
  green; terra-
  cotta orange;
  dark pink; light
  pink; purple;
  golden yellow
Stencils: bee; ½"
  checkerboard;
  dirt mound;
  fence; flower-
  pots; flowers;
  spade

Garden Lamp

Here's How:

1. Refer to Preparing Unfinished Wood on page 21. Prepare the wood.

2. Using flat brush, paint body of lamp with dark brown paint. Allow to dry.

3. Following manufacturer's instructions, paint over brown paint with crackle medium.

4. Paint over crackle medium with ivory paint. Allow to crackle and dry.

5. Spray the back side of checkerboard stencil with spray adhesive. Adhere stencil onto one side of the lower portion of body, just above base piece.

6. Refer to Stencilling Order on pages 23–24. Using stencil brushes, apply light blue paint into the openings of stencil to create two rows of checkerboard. Remove stencil and allow to dry. Repeat for each side.

7. Repeat Steps 5 and 6 for the upper portion of body, just below top piece.

8. Using flat brush, paint top and base of lamp with light blue paint.

9. Using sandpaper, sand all edges of lamp.

10. Spray lamp with matte acrylic spray. Allow to dry.

11. Carefully mist the edges lamp with antiquing spray. Allow to dry.

12. Repeat Step 10.

13. Spray the back side of fence post stencil. Adhere stencil onto lamp shade as desired.

14. Using a stencil brush, apply stencil creme into the openings of stencil. Remove stencil and allow to dry.

15. Repeat Steps 13 and 14 for remaining stencils, one at a time to build the scene.

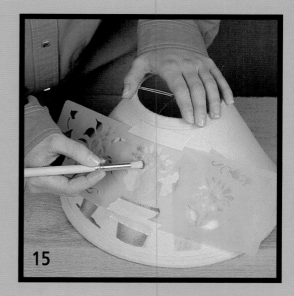

15

16. Assemble lamp kit in lamp.

Troubleshooting:

Avoid uneven spacing between images when stencilling around the lamp shade. Measure the available space or make a mock up first.

13
technique

What You Need to Get Started:

Acrylic paints:
  light blue; ivory
Applicators: fabric
  dye brushes;
  1" flat brush
Craft knife
Disposable palette
Masking tape: ¾"
  wide
Paper towels
Pencil
Sandpaper
Self-adhesive notes
Stencil cremes:
  colonial blue;
  brown; olive
  green; lavender;
  golden yellow
Stencil spray
  adhesive
Theorem stencil
  kit: morning
  glory vine
Wooden table:
  small

How do I use theorem stencils?

Theorem (multi-overlay) stencilling results in a hand-painted look. This technique yields a free-flowing design and soft lines. At first glance, it may seem like a complicated process, but it is actually very easy.

Morning Glory Table

Here's How:
1. Refer to Preparing Unfinished Wood on page 21. Prepare the wood.

2. Refer to Base-coating on page 22. Using a sponge brush, base-coat top and legs of table with ivory paint. Allow to dry.

3. Tape along each edge of top of table. Using craft knife, square corners of tape.

4. Using a sponge brush, paint the top edges, leg edges, center brace, and front and back sections of table with light blue paint. Allow to dry.

5. Using sandpaper, sand along the edges of table.

6. Spray the back sides of stencils with spray adhesive. Beginning with stencil #1, center and adhere stencil onto one side of table.

7. To mark registration marks, slide a self-adhesive note under hole in stencil, making certain note is not showing through any stencil openings. Using pencil, mark through hole onto note. Repeat for all registration marks on stencil #1.

8. Refer to Stencilling Order on pages 23–24. Using fabric dye brushes, apply stencil cremes, beginning with the lightest shade and working toward the darkest, into the openings of stencil. Remove stencil, taking care not to remove any registration notes, and allow to dry.

9. Carefully mist stencilled areas with matte acrylic spray. Allow to dry.

10. Adhere next stencil in sequence, lining up registration marks, and repeat Steps 8 and 9. Continue in this manner until all stencils have been used.

11. Repeat Steps 6 through 10 for remaining side and top of table.

12. Spray entire table with matte acrylic spray.

Tips:

If a small amount of paint seeps under the stencil edge, use a clean eraser to carefully daub the paint away. Be very careful not to smear the main design. This must be done before misting with matte acrylic spray.

If the kit you purchased has pattern lines to line up on each layer, those will likely be better registration marks since they are actually part of the design. Refer to them for accuracy.

Troubleshooting:

Lightly misting the stencilled area with matte acrylic spray helps avoid smearing between layers. This will also help keep the paint from sticking to the back of the next adhesive-sprayed stencil.

How can I stencil a wall border?

Stencilled borders can become a focal point in a room. Just make certain that the reason it is a focal point is because the stencilling was done correctly. Before beginning to stencil a room, consider the placement of the stencil—for a ceiling line border or frieze, a chair rail border, a vertical border, or a kickplate border.

What You Need to Get Started:

Applicators: fabric dye brushes
Carpenter's level
Chalk pencil
Disposable palette
Eraser
Matte acrylic spray
Paper towels
Self-adhesive notes
Stencil cremes: dark brown; light brown; olive green; dark pink; light pink; golden yellow
Stencil spray adhesive
Sturdy ladder
Theorem stencil kit: magnolia wall border
Yardstick

Magnolia Wall Border

Here's How:

1. Refer to Preparing Walls on page 21. Prepare the wall.

2. Determine the type of border that will be stencilled.

Ceiling Line Border or Frieze: This border is placed approximately 1" from the ceiling or crown molding. The border for a standard room should be at least 6" wide. If the chosen stencil design is not that wide, consider enlarging the design area by doubling the border or by adding a straight border edge to make up the width.

Chair Rail Border: This border is either placed just above or below the existing chair rail molding or actually takes the place of the molding. Chair rails are usually placed 32"–36" from the floor. As this is typically a narrower border, the stencil design should be approximately 3"–4" wide. However, in a larger, more spacious room, where the ceiling may be higher than 8', a wider border could be considered. Note: Chair rail borders should be level—even if the floor is not.

Kickplate Border: This border is about the same width as the chair rail border and is placed approximately ½"–1" above the existing baseboard.

Vertical Border: It is relatively easy to alter a stencil design to create a border to frame an architectural structure such as a large window or doorway. Note: Avoid this style of border if the corners of the structure are out of plumb as the stencilling would only draw more attention to this architectural flaw.

3. Measure the appropriate distance from ceiling, floor, or architectural structure for desired border. Using level and chalk pencil, draw a horizontal line on each wall or around structure in the room.

4. Determine the order in which the wall will be stencilled. Read and understand all manufacturer's instructions in stencil kit. For each layer that is to be painted, there are corresponding numbers labeling each stencil.

5. Spray the back sides of stencils with spray adhesive. Beginning with stencil

#1, adhere stencil onto wall. Align horizontal centering line, printed on stencil, with chalk line on wall. Erase any chalk lines that show through stencil openings. Note: If the stencil does not have a horizontal centering line, create one with a ruler and permanent marking pen.

6. To mark registration marks, slide a self-adhesive note under hole in stencil, making certain note is not showing through any stencil openings. Using pencil, mark through hole onto note. Repeat for all registration marks on stencil #1.

7. Refer to Stencilling Order on pages 23–24. Using fabric dye brushes, apply stencil cremes, beginning with the lightest shade and working toward the darkest, into the openings of stencil. Remove stencil, taking care not to remove any registration notes, and allow to dry.

8. Carefully mist stencilled areas with matte acrylic spray. Allow to dry.

9. Adhere the next stencil in the sequence, lining up registration marks, and repeat Steps 5 and 6. Continue in this manner until all stencils have been used.

10. Repeat Steps 3 through 7 to complete length of border.

11. After stencilling is complete and allowed to dry, erase any remaining chalk lines.

Tips:

Use only a few styles of borders per room. Once draperies, pictures, and other decorative accessories are back in place, determine whether additional motifs should be added as well. Stencilling can be a wonderful tool in decorating a room, but take care not to overdo it.

Stencilling can be used in rooms that have architectural problems such as windows and doors that are not level and walls and ceilings that are not plumb. Stencilling can actually disguise the flaws that were built into the house.

For a chair rail border, if there is already an existing chair rail molding, place the stencil along the top of the molding. Check to make certain that the design openings are approximately ½"–1" above the molding. If they are, this is the simplest way to measure and maintain consistent distance from the molding. Simply move the stencil along the molding.

Section 3: *projects beyond the basics*

How do I stencil on fabric?

Stencilling on fabric is so easy and perfectly suited to decorating a room. This technique adds soft lines and great design to pillows, tablecloths, curtains, and floor mats.

What You Need to Get Started:

Acrylic paints:
  ivory
Applicators:
  makeup sponges
Butcher paper:
  14½" x 38½"
Cardboard:
  15" x 39"
Disposable palette
Fabrics: waffle-
  textured 14½" x
  38½" (2); cotton
  3½" x 38½" (2);
  cotton 3½" x 19"
  (2)
Iron and ironing
  board
Natural batting:
  14½" x 38½"
Paper towels
Pencil
Ruler
Sewing machine
Stencil cremes:
  dark brown;
  reddish brown;
  olive green;
  terra-cotta
  orange; rustic
  red; golden
  yellow
Stencil spray
  adhesive
Stencil tape
Stencils: assorted
  leaves and
  berries; tile
Thread:
  coordinating

Autumn Leaf Table Runner

Here's How:

1. Refer to Preparing Fabric on page 22. Using iron, press fabric to remove wrinkles.

2. Using ruler and pencil, draw an outside line ¼" from each edge of cardboard to help when placing fabric onto cardboard.

3. Lightly spray cardboard with spray adhesive.

4. Lay one piece of waffle-textured fabric right side up on cardboard within outside line. Smooth fabric, taking care not to stretch it.

5. Using pencil and stencils, make a mock-up of the table runner design on a piece of butcher paper to ensure placement of stencils. Place mock-up nearby for easy reference.

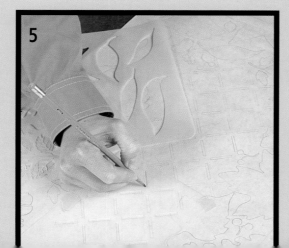

6. Center and trace an 18" x 36" rectangle onto waffle-textured fabric.

7. Tape tile stencil onto the center of rectangle.

8. Refer to Stencilling Order on pages 23–24. Using makeup sponges, apply ivory paint into the openings of stencil. Move stencil and repeat as necessary to fill length of rectangle and create a background.

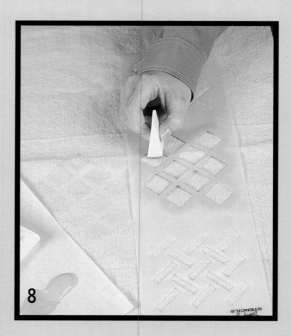

9. Apply assorted colors of stencil creme, beginning with the lightest shade and working toward the darkest, into the openings of leaf and berry stencils around each edge of

rectangle, overlapping pencil line approximately ½". Allow to dry 24 hours. Remove stencilled fabric from cardboard.

10. Place the remaining piece of waffle-textured fabric wrong side up on work surface. Place batting on top of fabric. Place stencilled fabric right side up on top of batting. Sew pieces together.

11. With right sides together, place cotton fabric strips along corresponding edges of stencilled fabric, 1¼" in from each edge.

12. Sew ¼" in from each edge of strips. Wrap fabric to the back of table runner, fold edge under ¼", and sew in place.

Tips:
Use the stencil tape to tape off unwanted leaves. This will solve the problem of paint in unwanted areas. This is especially important as it is difficult to remove unwanted paint from fabric.

Try mixing colors to create new shades. Refer to the photograph for varying colors of the yellows and greens which were mixed with small amounts of brown to create duller colors.

Troubleshooting:
Avoid using stencil adhesive to adhere

stencils to fabric as the stencil is often flipped for a reverse image.

Before flipping any stencil, make certain it is wiped clean to avoid unwanted paint on the table runner.

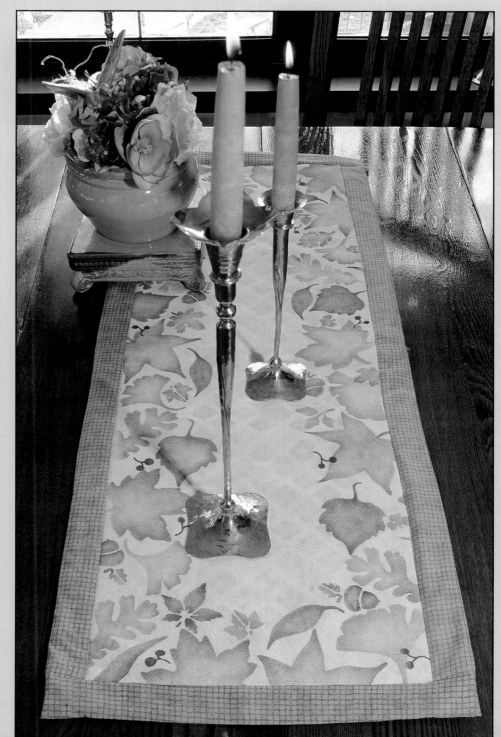

2 project

What You Need to Get Started:

Air-dry enamel
   paints: green;
   light green;
   dark red; red
Applicators: small
   sponge pouncers
Cling stencils: large
   rose; small rose
Disposable palette
Glass box
Paper towels

How do I stencil on glass?

Stencils made specifically for stencilling on glass make this technique quick and easy. Because the material from which they are made sticks to glass surfaces, they are called "cling stencils." A wide variety of paints that are durable enough for glass, tile, and ceramic are also available. The combination of these tools and materials leaves endless opportunity for using this technique.

Rose Box

Here's How:

1. Refer to Preparing Glassware on page 22. Prepare the glass.

2. Place large rose stencil on the center of glass box lid.

3. Refer to Stencilling Order on pages 23–24. Using small sponge pouncers, apply paint, beginning with the lightest shade and working toward the darkest, into the openings of stencil. Remove stencil and allow to dry.

4. For each side panel of box, place small rose stencil on center of glass.

5. Repeat Step 3 for side panels.

Tip:
The fewer the layers the better. Cling stencils are easier to remove when a heavy build-up of paint can be avoided.

After each use of the stencil, clean it with cling stencil cleanser.

Troubleshooting:
Avoid too many layers. Allow the paint to dry between layers. The paint is "sticky" and tends to pick up the previous layer if it is not dry.

3
project

How do I stencil on ceramic tile?

What You Need to Get Started:

Acrylic paint:
  dark green
Adhesive for tiles
Air-dry enamel
  paints: brown;
  orange
Applicators:
  1" flat brush;
  makeup sponges
Ceramic tiles:
  white, blank (2);
  white, numbered
  for your address
Disposable palette
Paper towels
Stencil: butterfly
Stencil spray
  adhesive
Wooden welcome
  sign

Stencilling on tile is just like stencilling on glass. Add this design element to the kitchen or bath—there are many different images from which to choose.

Butterfly Welcome Sign

Here's How:
1. Refer to Preparing Unfinished Wood on page 21. Prepare the wood.

2. Using flat brush, paint sign's frame with dark green paint. Allow to dry.

3. Using sandpaper, sand along the edges of frame.

4. Spray frame with matte acrylic spray.

5. Spray the back side of stencil with spray adhesive. Adhere stencil onto one blank tile.

6. Refer to Stencilling Order on pages 23–24. Using makeup sponges, apply air-dry enamel paints, beginning with the lightest shade and working toward the darkest, into the openings of stencil. Remove stencil and allow to dry.

7. Repeat Steps 5 and 6 for remaining blank tile.

8. Using tile adhesive, adhere tiles into frame.

4
project

What You Need to Get Started:

Acrylic paint:
  brown
Applicators:
  makeup sponges;
  sponge brushes
Craft scissors
Disposable palette
Paper towels
Outdoor paints:
  colonial blue;
  dark colonial
  blue; brown;
  dark brown;
  dark green;
  olive green;
  ivory; terra-
  cotta orange;
  dark pink; light
  pink; tan; white;
  golden yellow
Stencil spray
  adhesive
Stencils: assorted
  for pots
Terra-cotta pots:
  8"; 6"; 4"
Toothbrush

There are specially made stencils, which are designed to wrap around the surface of a terra-cotta pot. Combined with outdoor paints that are now available, pots and other garden accents can be decorated with paint that is weatherproof and fade-resistant.

Garden Pots

Here's How:

1. Refer to Base-coating on page 22. Using a sponge brush, base-coat body of large and small pots with ivory paint. Allow to dry.

2. Using a sponge brush, base-coat body of medium pot with tan paint. Allow to dry.

3. Using a sponge brush, base-coat rim and base of large pot with olive green paint. Allow to dry.

4. Using a sponge brush, base-coat rim and base of medium pot with brown paint. Allow to dry.

5. Using a sponge brush, base-coat rim and base of small pot with terra-cotta orange paint. Allow to dry.

6. Using craft scissors and following manufacturer's instructions, cut out stencil to fit around pot.

7. For each pot, spray the back side of stencil with spray adhesive. Wrap and adhere stencil onto pot.

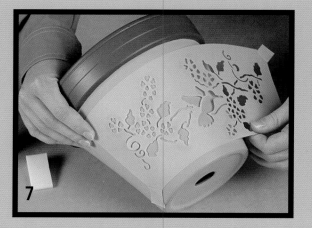

8. Refer to Stencilling Order on pages 23–24. Using makeup sponges, apply paints, beginning with the lightest shade and working toward the darkest, into the openings of stencil. Repeat the design around pot as desired. Remove stencil and allow to dry.

9. For the small pot, adhere a small stencil onto rim. Using makeup sponges, apply paint into the openings of stencil. Repeat design as desired. Remove stencil and allow to dry.

10. For an antiqued look, load a small amount of brown acrylic paint, thinned with a little water, onto toothbrush. Holding brush over pot, bristles down,

pull thumb slowly across bristles. This causes the paint to spatter. Repeat for each pot.

Tips:

Base-coat at least half way down inside the pots. A nice clean edge is much more attractive and is much easier to paint without worrying about making a straight edge at the top of the rim.

When spattering the pots, make certain to use acrylic paint thinned with a little water. The outdoor paint is of a sticky consistency and will produce stringy spattering.

Troubleshooting:

Make certain the pots sit for a while to allow for curing before stencilling. Sometimes the spray adhesive will pull up the base-coat paint.

Make certain to apply the paint in thin layers to avoid seeping under the stencil.

Stencils specially made for pots may not fit all pots perfectly. If this is the case, work around the pot, stencilling small areas at a time.

How do I stencil on tin?

Simple stencil designs combined with an interesting tin object result in a piece that will be prized for years to come.

What You Need to Get Started:

Acrylic paints:
  black; dark green;
  ivory; dark red
Antiquing spray
Applicators:
  makeup sponges;
  sponge brushes
Disposable palette
Matte acrylic spray
Paper towels
Stencil cremes:
  black; light blue;
  dark green; olive
  green; pale
  green; terra-
  cotta orange;
  pink; red;
  golden yellow
Stencil spray
  adhesive
Stencils: "herb
  garden"; herbs
Tin watering can
Toothbrush

Herb Watering Can

Here's How:

1. Refer to Preparing Tin on page 22. Prepare the tin.

2. Refer to Base-coating on page 22. Using a sponge brush, base-coat body, spout, and topside of handles of watering can with ivory paint. Allow to dry.

3. Using a sponge brush, base-coat underside of handles, nozzle, rim, and base of watering can with dark red paint. Allow to dry.

4. Using a sponge brush, base-coat band around watering can with dark green paint. Allow to dry.

5. Spray the back side of "herb garden" stencil with spray adhesive. Adhere stencil onto body of watering can just below green band.

6. Refer to Stencilling Order on pages 23–24. Using a makeup sponge, apply red paint into the openings of stencil. Remove stencil and allow to dry.

7. Spray the back side of herbs stencil with spray adhesive. Adhere stencil onto body of watering can just below green band.

8. Using makeup sponges, apply stencil cremes into the openings of stencil. Remove stencil and allow to dry.

9. For an antiqued look, load a small amount of thinned black acrylic paint onto toothbrush. Holding brush over watering can, bristles down, pull thumb across bristles. This causes paint to spatter.

10. Spray entire watering can with matte acrylic spray. Allow to dry.

11. Carefully mist watering can with antiquing spray. Allow to dry.

12. Repeat Step 10.

Tip:
Because the watering can is rounded, it may be easier to stencil each herb motif individually.

Troubleshooting:
Avoid overspraying when using the antiquing spray. Light coats are recommended for even coverage. Practice using the spray before applying it to the project.

A rub-on antiquing gel may be easier to work with and can be used instead of the antiquing spray.

6 project

What You Need to Get Started:

Applicator:
  makeup sponge
Concrete stepping
  stone
Disposable palette
Outdoor paint:
  dark green
Paper towels
Pencil
Ruler
Self-adhesive notes
Stencil: scrolls
Stencil spray
  adhesive

How do I stencil on concrete?

Simple outdoor decorative accents such as stepping stones can be enhanced with stencilling. Paint a little ivy or some lattice to brighten up the path or flower garden.

Concrete Stepping Stone

Here's How:
1. Refer to Preparing Concrete on page 22. Prepare the concrete.

2. Using ruler, measure stepping stone to find center of length of each side and of entire stone.

3. Using pencil and self-adhesive notes, mark center points. Transfer any registration marks onto stone.

4. Spray the back side of stencil with spray adhesive. Center and adhere stencil onto stepping stone within length of one side.

5. Refer to Stencilling Order on pages 23–24. Using makeup sponge, apply paint into openings of stencil. Carefully remove stencil without disturbing self-adhesive notes and allow to dry.

6. Repeat Steps 4 and 5 for each side of stepping stone.

How do I combine and embellish stencil motifs?

A combination of stencils and a little hand-painting can go a long way in completing a project such as these stacked tins. Layering the stencil motifs results in an antique look.

What You Need to Get Started:

Acrylic paints:
  brownish black;
  colonial blue;
  dark olive green;
  dark ivory; ivory;
  rustic orange;
  rusty red;
  golden yellow
Antiquing spray
Applicators: #3
  liner brush;
  sponge brushes;
  stencil brushes
Disposable palette
Lining pen: brown
Matte acrylic spray
Nested tins (3)
Paper towels
Stencil spray
  adhesive
Stencil tape
Stencils: ¼"
  checkerboard;
  1" checkerboard;
  chicken and
  eggs; large
  sunflower;
  small sunflower;
  vegetable pot;
  "vegetables";
  vegetables

Tri-stacked Tins

Here's How:

1. Refer to Preparing Tin on page 22. Prepare the tins.

2. Refer to Base-coating on page 22. Using a sponge brush, base-coat body of medium tin and lids of large and small tins with ivory paint. Allow to dry.

3. Using a sponge brush, base-coat body of large and small tins and lid of medium tin with colonial blue paint. Allow to dry.

4. Using a sponge brush, base-coat band around lid and bottom lip of large tin with rusty red paint. Allow to dry.

5. Using a sponge brush, base-coat lip of lid of large tin with dark olive green paint. Allow to dry.

6. Using a sponge brush, base-coat band around lid of medium tin with brownish black paint. Allow to dry.

7. Using a sponge brush, base-coat lip of lid and bottom lip of medium tin with colonial blue paint. Allow to dry.

8. Using a sponge brush, base-coat band around lid and bottom lip of small tin with dark olive green paint. Allow to dry.

9. Using a sponge brush, base-coat lip of lid of small tin with dark ivory paint. Allow to dry.

10. Spray the back side of 1" checkerboard stencil with spray adhesive. Adhere stencil onto lid of large tin.

11. Refer to Stencilling Order on pages 23–24. Using a makeup sponge, apply colonial blue paint into the openings of stencil. Remove the stencil and allow to dry.

12. Repeat Steps 10 and 11 for lid of small tin.

13. Repeat Steps 10 and 11, using ivory paint, for lid of medium tin.

14. Spray the back sides of large sunflower, vegetable pot, and chicken and eggs stencils with spray adhesive. Adhere large sunflower onto lid of large tin, vegetable pot onto lid of medium tin, and chicken and eggs onto lid of small tin.

15. Using makeup sponges, apply assorted colors of paint into the openings of stencils. Remove stencils and allow to dry.

16. Spray the back side of "vegetables" stencil with spray adhesive. Adhere stencil onto lid of medium tin just above stencilled vegetable pot.

17. Using makeup sponges, apply rusty red paint into the openings of stencil. Remove stencil and allow to dry.

18. Spray the back side of ¼" checkerboard stencil with spray adhesive. Adhere stencil onto lid of small tin just below stencilled chicken and eggs. Tape off the openings that overlap stencilled chicken and eggs.

19. Using makeup sponges, apply brownish black paint into the openings of stencil to create two rows of checkerboard. Remove stencil and allow to dry.

20. Adhere stencil onto body of small tin just above bottom lip.

21. Using makeup sponges, apply rusty red paint into the openings of stencil to create two rows of checkerboard. Remove stencil and allow to dry.

22. Tape off half of small sunflower stencil. Spray the back side of stencil with spray adhesive. Adhere stencil onto body of small tin just above stencilled checkerboard.

23. Using makeup sponges, apply brownish black and golden yellow paint into the openings of stencil. Remove stencil and allow to dry.

24. Remove tape from small sunflower stencil. Center and adhere stencil onto body of large tin.

25. Repeat Step 23.

26. Spray the back side of vegetable stencils with spray adhesive. Adhere stencils onto body of medium tin.

27. Using makeup sponges, apply paint into openings of stencils. Remove stencils and allow to dry.

28. Using liner brush, apply thinned ivory paint onto small sunflowers on large and small tins, creating a plaid.

29. Using lining pen, draw "stitch" marks around stencilled 1" checkerboard on each lid, around top of body of large and small tins, around bottom of body of large tin, around

small sunflower centers on large and small tins, and around vegetables on body of medium tin.

30. Spray each tin with matte acrylic spray. Allow to dry.

31. Carefully mist the edges of each tin with antiquing spray. Allow to dry.

32. Repeat Step 30.

8
project

What You Need to Get Started:

Acrylic paints:
  colonial blue;
  brown; dark
  green; rustic red;
  dark yellow;
  golden yellow;
  light yellow
Adhesive: industrial
  strength
Antiquing spray
Applicators: #3
  liner brush;
  makeup sponges;
  sponge brushes
Clockworks
Disposable palette
Lining pen: brown
Matte acrylic spray
Paper towels
Resin or wooden
  decorative
  accents:
  birdhouses (4);
  sunflowers (5)
Sandpaper
Stencil spray
  adhesive
Stencils: ⅜"
  checkerboard;
  ½" checkerboard
Wooden birdhouse
  clock

How can I get the most out of a simple stencil?

Use color to achieve different effects with one stencil. A simple stencil such as the checkerboard can become a great design element when it is used with contrasting colors to create a background. This project is sure to catch the eye.

Birdhouse Clock

Here's How:

1. Refer to Preparing Unfinished Wood on page 21. Prepare the wood.

2. Refer to Base-coating on page 22. Using a sponge brush, base-coat roof and pendulum back board with colonial blue paint. Allow to dry.

3. Using a sponge brush, base-coat clock front with light yellow paint. Allow to dry.

4. Using a sponge brush, base-coat clock face and birdhouse sides with dark yellow paint. Allow to dry.

5. Using a sponge brush, paint opening edge of clock front, and bottom edge of clock front with rustic red paint. Allow to dry.

6. Spray the back side of ⅜" checkerboard stencil with spray adhesive. Adhere stencil onto pendulum back board.

7. Refer to Stencilling Order on pages 23–24. Using a makeup sponge, apply rustic red paint into the openings of stencil to create two rows of checker-board. Remove stencil and allow to dry.

8. Spray the back side of ½" checkerboard stencil with spray adhesive. Adhere stencil onto clock front.

9. Using a makeup sponge, apply dark yellow paint into the openings of stencil. Remove stencil and allow to dry.

10. Reposition and adhere stencil onto clock face.

11. Using a makeup sponge, apply colonial blue paint into the openings of stencil. Remove stencil and allow to dry.

12. Using liner brush, paint stems and leaves in varying heights onto pendulum back board with dark green paint.

13. Using sandpaper, sand along the edges of roof and pendulum back board.

14. Using lining pen, draw "stitch" marks around the edge of pendulum back board.

15. Using a sponge brush, paint body of each birdhouse decorative accent with dark green paint. Allow to dry.

16. Using a sponge brush, paint roof and base of each bird-house decorative accent with rustic red paint. Allow to dry.

17. Using a sponge brush, paint petals of each sunflower decorative accent with golden yellow paint. Allow to dry.

18. Using a sponge brush, paint center of each sunflower decorative accent with brown paint. Allow to dry.

19. Spray decorative accents with antiquing spray. Allow to dry.

20. Adhere birdhouse decorative accents onto clock front at 12, 3, 6, and 9 around clock face with industrial strength adhesive.

21. Adhere sunflower decorative accents onto pendulum back board at top of each painted stem.

22. Spray birdhouse clock with matte acrylic spray. Allow to dry.

23. Carefully mist the edges with antiquing spray. Allow to dry.

24. Repeat Step 22.

25. Attach clockworks to clock face.

Tip:
   If possible, remove the clock face for painting and stencilling.

9
project

What You Need to Get Started:

Acrylic paint: ivory
Applicators:
  1" flat brush;
  sponge brush;
  stencil brushes
Card stock
Craft knife
Cutting mat
Disposable palette
Glass hurricane: 10"
Matte acrylic spray
Paper towels
Stencil: iris and
  hollyhock
Stencil cremes:
  colonial blue;
  olive green;
  dark pink; pink;
  purple; yellow
Stencil spray
  adhesive
Wooden block:
  5¼" x 5¼" x 4"
  with a centered
  3" circle drilled
  ½" deep

Large border stencils can also work on a small surface. The entire stencil design does not have to fit a particular space. Portions of the iris and hollyhock stencil work great around this block of wood.

English Garden Hurricane Base

Here's How:
1. Refer to Preparing Unfinished Wood on page 21. Prepare the wood.

2. Refer to Base-coating on page 22. Using sponge brush, base-coat wooden block with ivory paint. Allow to dry.

3. One side at a time, position stencil as desired for varied images.

4. Spray the back side of stencil with spray adhesive. Adhere stencil onto one side of wooden block.

5. Refer to Stencilling Order on pages 23–24. Using stencil brushes, apply stencil cremes, beginning with the lightest shade and working toward the darkest, into the openings of stencil. Remove stencil and allow to dry.

6. Spray stencilled side with matte acrylic spray. Allow to dry.

7. Repeat Steps 3 through 6 for remaining sides of wooden block.

8. Using craft knife, cut a 3½" circle from card stock, leaving a circle stencil.

9. Spray the back side of card stock stencil with spray adhesive.

10. Adhere card stock stencil onto top of wooden block so drilled circle is centered within stencil opening.

11. Using stencil brushes, apply pink paint into the opening of stencil. Remove stencil and allow to dry.

12. Spray entire wooden block with matte acrylic spray. Allow to dry.

13. Set glass hurricane into drilled circle.

10 project

How can I display my stencilled projects?

Turn beautiful stencilled projects into framed works of art.
Use a shadow box to add character, dimension, and interest.

What You Need to Get Started:

Acrylic paint:
  sage green
Applicators:
  sponge brush;
  stencil brushes
Custom-made mat
Disposable palette
Mat boards: 6" x 8"
  (2)
Matte acrylic spray
Stencil: pear
Stencil cremes:
  dark brown;
  reddish brown;
  olive green;
  orange pink;
  pink; golden
  yellow; sun-
  flower yellow
Stencil spray
  adhesive
Stencil tape
Wooden frame
  shadow box: 8"
  x 20" unfinished

Framed Pears

Here's How:

1. Refer to Preparing Unfinished Wood on page 21. Prepare the frame.

2. Using a sponge brush, paint frame with sage green paint. Allow to dry.

3. Using sandpaper, sand along the edges of frame.

4. Spray frame with matte acrylic spray.

5. Spray the back side of stencil with spray adhesive. Adhere stencil onto one mat board.

6. Refer to Stencilling Order on pages 23–24. Using stencil brushes, apply stencil cremes, beginning with the lightest shade and working toward the darkest, into the openings of stencil. Remove stencil and allow to dry.

7. Repeat Steps 5 and 6 for remaining mat board.

8. Assemble stencilled mat boards in custom-made mat and frame.

Tips:

Use a separate brush for each color of stencil creme to avoid muddy colors.

Do not forget to add pinks into the leaves and pears.

Troubleshooting:

Take care when placing the custom-made mat on the stencilled mat boards to avoid smearing the stencil cremes.

designed by Sheri Hoeger

designed by Stacey Flowers

designed by Sheri Hoeger

designed by Sheri Hoeger

designed by Stacey Flowers

Section 4: *gallery*

designed by Sheri Hoeger

designed by Sheri Hoeger

Lynn Brehm has been designing and painting stencils and murals in San Diego, California, for 15 years. She sells her designs through her own mail order stencil catalog, Natural Accents. She also distributes to several retail stencil shops across the United States and has her own website, www.natural-accents.com.

A teacher and member of the Stencil Artisans League, Inc. (SALI), Lynn is also the president of the online chapter, Stenciling Round Table. She cofounded a local chapter of SALI, Stencil Artisans of San Diego, in 1994.

Lynn lives in Carlsbad, California, with her daughter, Megan, and their two cats.

designed by Lynn Brehm

designed by Lynn Brehm

designed by Lynn Brehm

designed by Lynn Brehm

Stacey Flowers owns and operates Grand Illusions, a decorative painting business based out of Fort Worth, Texas. She holds a degree from the Fashion Institute of Technology in New York. While there, she studied fashion design, textile technology, interior design, marketing, and advertising. She is also a member of the Stencil Artisan's League, Inc., and the Society of Decorative Painters.

Stacey's creative endeavors focus mainly on murals, freeform stencilling, trompe l'oeil, and designer paint finishes. She also enjoys teaching and demonstrating these techniques. She is very excited about the emergence of the new, more sophisticated stencil designs available in today's market. She uses this "new breed" of stencils as a tool to create richly shaded three-dimensional elements in all of her work, whether it be a mural or some smaller vignette.

Stacey lives by this motto: "Life is a great big canvas and you should throw all the paint on it you can."

designed by Stacey Flowers

designed by Stacey Flowers

designed by Stacey Flowers

94

designed by Stacey Flowers

Shortly after **Sheri Hoeger** began stencilling professionally, her son, Justin, exclaimed, "You are like a mad scientist, only with stencilling . . . you're the mad stencilist!" Since 1988, Sheri's decorative painting techniques and designs have been gracing residences, show homes, and anything else that doesn't move too fast. Her work has been featured in magazines, books, and on television. She has gained a national reputation for her original designs and shading techniques. She shares her knowledge by teaching workshops in California and at the annual Stencil Artisans League, Inc. convention.

designed by Sheri Hoeger

designed by Sheri Hoeger

designed by Sheri Hoeger

designed by Sheri Hoeger

designed by L.A. Stencilworks

Barbara Robins and business partner, **Cynthia Willoughby**, have actively worked in the field of stencilling since the early 1980s.

As long-time members of the Southern California decorative painting community, they have used stencilling and faux finishing to decorate walls. They have also used these techniques to decorate furniture and for painting small wall murals.

As they developed numerous stencil designs for their clients, it became apparent to the two women that their designs could fill a void that existed in the stencil market. In 1997, they joined forces and L.A. Stencilworks was born. Three years later they have more than 500 stencil designs that range from classic scrollwork to more than 200 trompe l'oeil elements.

Barbara and Cynthia have participated in many classes to learn new techniques for stencilling, faux finishing, and decorative painting. They have been invited on several occasions to teach at retail decorative painting shops and through community college programs.

designed by L.A. Stencilworks

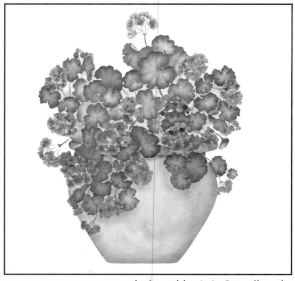

designed by L.A. Stencilworks

designed by L.A. Stencilworks

designed by L.A. Stencilworks

designed by L.A. Stencilworks

designed by L.A. Stencilworks

designed by L.A. Stencilworks

designed by L.A. Stencilworks

102

Nora Marie Moeller was born and raised in Northern California. Educated in art and interior design, she began using stencils in 1983 in conjunction with other forms of art. She is a member of the Stencil Artisans League, Inc. Her work has been published in the *Artistic Stenciler* magazine.

Nora has been stencilling professionally since 1987. She started out stencilling on children's furniture. The work was relatively simple and her young customers were almost always satisfied. However, the current demand for professional

designed by Nora Moeller

stencilling requires much more creativity. Her work now consists of carefully coordinating stencils to create murals of all sizes and beautiful trompe l'oeil embellishments.

Nora has designed many of her own stencils to suit the needs of her clients and also uses many of the designer stencils available on the market. She consistently uses these stencils to decorate many different surfaces such as tiles, kitchen cabinets, and of course, walls.

Nora also stencils on furniture and has displayed many of her pieces at home and art shows in her area. She has also developed a website for her clients to view her work.

designed by Nora Moeller

103

designed by Nora Moeller

designed by Nora Moeller

designed by Nora Moeller

Melanie Royals, as an artist and stencil designer, is driven by her goal to be a continual force in changing the common perception that stencilling is primitive, unimaginative, uncreative, and unsophisticated.

After 15 years of constant interest and experimentation, her focus remains on using stencils in new and innovative ways while utilizing a wide variety of materials and techniques.

Similarly, the goal of Melanie's company, Royal Design Studio, is to provide sophisticated stencil designs that are simple to complete yet challenge the creativity of the user by their versatility.

Melanie takes the time to share her knowledge and experience with her students through workshops held at the San Diego School of Decorative Arts, as well as other fine decorative painting institutions across the United States.

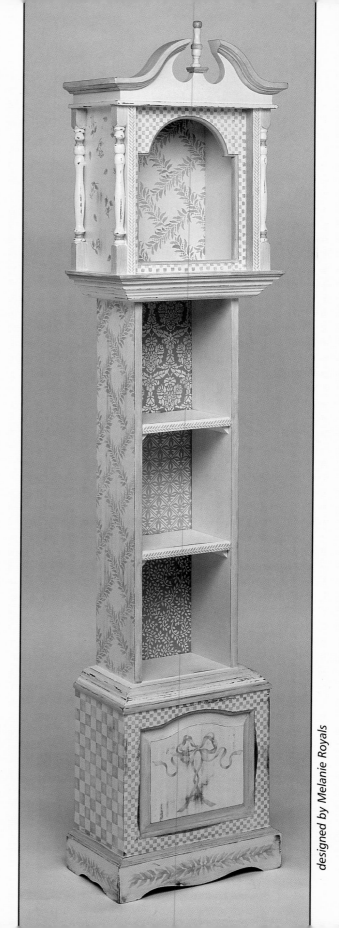

designed by Melanie Royals

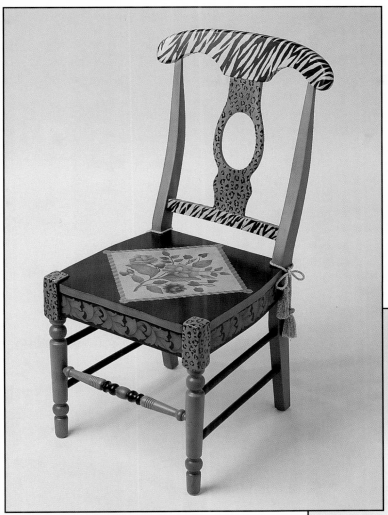

designed by Melanie Royals

designed by Melanie Royals

107

designed by Melanie Royals

por siempre jamás

designed by Melanie Royals

Metric equivalency chart

mm-millimetres cm-centimetres
inches to millimetres and centimetres

inches	mm	cm	inches	cm	inches	cm
⅛	3	0.3	9	22.9	30	76.2
¼	6	0.6	10	25.4	31	78.7
⅜	10	1.0	11	27.9	32	81.3
½	13	1.3	12	30.5	33	83.8
⅝	16	1.6	13	33.0	34	86.4
¾	19	1.9	14	35.6	35	88.9
⅞	22	2.2	15	38.1	36	91.4
1	25	2.5	16	40.6	37	94.0
1¼	32	3.2	17	43.2	38	96.5
1½	38	3.8	18	45.7	39	99.1
1¾	44	4.4	19	48.3	40	101.6
2	51	5.1	20	50.8	41	104.1
2½	64	6.4	21	53.3	42	106.7
3	76	7.6	22	55.9	43	109.2
3½	89	8.9	23	58.4	44	111.8
4	102	10.2	24	61.0	45	114.3
4½	114	11.4	25	63.5	46	116.8
5	127	12.7	26	66.0	47	119.4
6	152	15.2	27	68.6	48	121.9
7	178	17.8	28	71.1	49	124.5
8	203	20.3	29	73.7	50	127.0

yards to metres

yards	metres	yards	metres	yards	metres	yards	metres	yards	metres
⅛	0.11	2⅛	1.94	4⅛	3.77	6⅛	5.60	8⅛	7.43
¼	0.23	2¼	2.06	4¼	3.89	6¼	5.72	8¼	7.54
⅜	0.34	2⅜	2.17	4⅜	4.00	6⅜	5.83	8⅜	7.66
½	0.46	2½	2.29	4½	4.11	6½	5.94	8½	7.77
⅝	0.57	2⅝	2.40	4⅝	4.23	6⅝	6.06	8⅝	7.89
¾	0.69	2¾	2.51	4¾	4.34	6¾	6.17	8¾	8.00
⅞	0.80	2⅞	2.63	4⅞	4.46	6⅞	6.29	8⅞	8.12
1	0.91	3	2.74	5	4.57	7	6.40	9	8.23
1⅛	1.03	3⅛	2.86	5⅛	4.69	7⅛	6.52	9⅛	8.34
1¼	1.14	3¼	2.97	5¼	4.80	7¼	6.63	9¼	8.46
1⅜	1.26	3⅜	3.09	5⅜	4.91	7⅜	6.74	9⅜	8.57
1½	1.37	3½	3.20	5½	5.03	7½	6.86	9½	8.69
1⅝	1.49	3⅝	3.31	5⅝	5.14	7⅝	6.97	9⅝	8.80
1¾	1.60	3¾	3.43	5¾	5.26	7¾	7.09	9¾	8.92
1⅞	1.71	3⅞	3.54	5⅞	5.37	7⅞	7.20	9⅞	9.03
2	1.83	4	3.66	6	5.49	8	7.32	10	9.14

Index